HODDER AND STOUGHTON'S PEOPLE'S LIBRARY

General Editor : Sidney Dark

VICTORIAN POETRY

BY
JOHN DRINKWATER

HODDER AND STOUGHTON LTD.
LONDON   TORONTO

General Preface

THE object of HODDER AND STOUGHTON'S PEOPLE'S LIBRARY is to supply in brief form simply written introductions to the study of History, Literature, Biography and Science; in some degree to satisfy that ever-increasing demand for knowledge which is one of the happiest characteristics of our time. The names of the authors of the first volumes of the Library are sufficient evidence of the fact that each subject will be dealt with authoritatively, while the authority will not be of the "dry-as-dust" order. Not only is it possible to have learning without tears, but it is also possible to make the acquiring of knowledge a thrilling and entertaining adventure. HODDER AND STOUGHTON'S PEOPLE'S LIBRARY will, it is hoped, supply this adventure.

Printed in Great Britain by R. Clay & Sons, Ltd., Bungay, Suffolk.

TO
GEORGE GORDON

A Summary

Introductory Note

THIS book is called *Victorian Poetry* for convenience. It does not, it need hardly be said, pretend to anything like a thorough examination of the voluminous poetry of the Victorian era in all its aspects. Significant criticism of Tennyson alone, to take a single instance, has already filled many volumes, a reflection which may well make the title chosen for this little book look like an impertinence. But while the present study does not profess to any exhaustiveness, it is about Victorian poetry, so that I may perhaps be allowed the choice, which is an easy one.

Certain omissions in the poets dealt with will occur to every reader. Chief of these, perhaps, is Mr. Thomas Hardy, but although Mr. Hardy might be claimed as at least partly Victorian in date he seems as a poet to belong to a later age in everything else. His own achievement is post-Victorian in character, and his influence upon the tradition of English poetry is one that is too presently active for definition yet awhile. So that I felt that to bring a consideration of his poetry into these notes would be to disturb the balance of the scheme. The same thing may be said, perhaps with rather less excuse, about George Meredith. He, more strictly than Mr. Hardy, belongs to the Victorian age, but it is by accident rather than by character. American poetry, save for a casual reference here and there, I have not mentioned at all. To have done so would not have furthered my design, nor could I have done it adequately within that design. Whitman, who is a law unto himself, could come into no design and needs a separate gospelling.

This brief study inevitably deals chiefly with the work of Tennyson, Browning, Arnold, Rossetti, Swinburne and Morris. Poets of almost equal eminence, such as Coventry Patmore, Mrs. Browning and Christina Rossetti, are less constant *motifs*, but, I hope, not unduly neglected. Of the great number of less cele-brated poets, who contributed beautifully to the poetry of their time, I have referred only to such as have afforded some apt illus-tration for an immediate argument. Poets like Landor and Emily Brontë, although they worked into the early part of the period dealt with, Landor, indeed, well into it, have not been treated as Victorians, since they belonged by nature no more to the Victorian age than did Wordsworth.

There could be no hard dividing line between the two parts of the study. Frequent references to the content matter of Victorian poetry were inevitable in a consideration of its technique, just as it has suited the argument often to refer back from the substance to the manner. For the rest, the main purpose of the essay has been merely to note some poetical characteristics of an age and their relation to the poetical characteristics of other ages.

I have used such terms as Augustan age and Romantic age as meaning what they are commonly held to mean in English criticism. That their fitness as terms may be sometimes challenged by critics of authority does not matter for the present purpose. They are convenient labels and may as well be used as any others. In choosing quotations for illustrative purposes, I have inclined when possible to such passages as are commonly known to readers of poetry, and since this book may be read by some who are not so erudite as my critics will be, I have thought it not superfluous to set out even so familiar a piece as *Crossing the Bar*, shall we say, in full.

Part I

I

THE division of poetry into periods is artificial and yet not without reason and its uses. If we look at the poets of an age at close quarters we shall commonly find little resemblance between one and the other. A liberal reader of poetry in 1670, for example, would be discussing the recently published *Paradise Lost*, he would know John Dryden as a poet who was establishing a reputation, he might still have bought from his booksellers the first edition of Herrick's *Hesperides* and have found on the poetry table the early issues of John Donne, Richard Crashaw, Henry King, Richard Lovelace and Henry Vaughan, among others. In these, his contemporaries, our reader would naturally see an immense variety of technical method, spiritual mood, and traditional allegiance. Cavalier and Puritan, secular and religious, these would be schools clearly distinguished in his mind, and little enough relation would be apparent between the monumental epic of Milton and the primrose lyric of Herrick. And yet these were all seventeenth-century poets, and at this distance we perceive something characteristic in seventeenth-century poetry that touched the work of all these men alike. We to-day are going through the same experience with our own contemporaries. Two hundred years hence Georgian poetry—and in this term I do not include only the work of the poets selected by Mr. Marsh for his anthologies—will have certain clearly definable characteristics which for the reader mark it apart from the work of other ages. And yet to us, if we really read the poetry and do not merely pick up a smattering of critical generalisation about it, the differences must be found more striking than the resemblances. At close quarters it is absurd to pretend that there is any close kinship between the work of, say, Mr. Lascelles Abercrombie, Mr. W. H. Davies, Mr. Walter de la Mare, Mr. John Masefield and Mr. Wilfred Wilson Gibson. What happens is that there are two governing influences in all poetry of any consequence, the poet's own personality, and the spirit of the age. That personality is something which is plain to a sensitive reader from the first, but the spirit of an age is hardly ever definable to the age itself. Criticism may already be sure about the personal quality in the work of Alice Meynell or A. E. Housman, can in some degree say why it is personal and mark in each case its particular contribution to the record of the human spirit, but criticism cannot clearly at present say what it is that relates these two poets to each other or both of them to Gordon Bottomley. That there is such a relation only becomes an established fact when we look back and see it asserting itself among the poets of a period from one age to another. Milton was a poet engaged in a titanic struggle with the problems of the soul, believing but battling always for his faith, blending in one mood a stern asceticism with voluptuous passion, a poetical technician familiar with every classic example and at the same time liberal in experiment; and just such a poet in his own measure was Matthew Arnold. Herrick, on the other hand, for all his parsonage, was the lyrist of fleeting beauty, of ghosts in the blossoming meadows, of exquisite and poignant moments, with no gospel but that with beauty loved comes beauty lost, a poet who used simple and established measures with perfect mastery and little questioning. And so again on his own scale such a poet was Swinburne. And yet in some essential respect Milton is of a kind with Herrick and Arnold of a kind with Swinburne far more clearly than is Milton with Arnold or Herrick with Swinburne. When the question of personal quality has been finally considered Milton and Herrick remain of the seventeenth century and Arnold and Swinburne of the nineteenth. The purpose of the present essay is to ascertain as far as possible what it is that distinguishes what we call the Victorian age in English poetry from the great ages that preceded it. In order to do this it will be necessary to consider the personal quality in several poets, but this will be done rather to discover the common spirit than to present a series of individual studies.

II

Queen Victoria came to the throne in 1837. The date is not an inconvenient one to set at the beginning of a study of the poetry of the age to which she gave her name. Shelley, Byron, and Keats were dead, Wordsworth's most important work was finished, Alfred Tennyson, Robert Browning, and Elizabeth Barrett had made their first appearances in print, Matthew Arnold was at school, Dante Gabriel Rossetti and his sister Christina were

children, William Morris and Algernon Charles
Swinburne had just been born. Walter Savage
Landor, one of the strangest figures in our
poetical literature, whose first poems had been
published in 1795, was still at the prime of
his genius, but the small body of his best work
does not mark him very definitely as either
Romantic or Victorian. There were a number
of less famous but by no means inconsiderable
poets whose work will call for notice as we
proceed.

The Romantic Revival in English poetry
is generally accepted as having Blake and Gray
and Collins for its pioneers. It must, however,
be remembered that the earlier part of the
eighteenth century, the age of reason, had not
been wholly without the Romantic note. To
read the work of the almost forgotten smaller
men of that time is to chance often upon a
phrase in which the tenderness, and heart-ache,
and the warm sense of colour and natural beauty,
which were so to dominate the great epoch
from Wordsworth to Keats, break through the
witty and balanced argument of an age when
it was not considered to be the thing to say
too much about the heart. Even the master,
Pope himself, in some of his pastorals and elegies,
and in such a poem as *Eloisa to Abelard*, sometimes lets the glow of passion play upon a poetic

habit that was not used to have its cold and logical brilliance ruffled except by anger. In those days, however, the romantic note when it was struck seems rather to have been struck by accident than by deliberation, while in Gray and Collins there is continually an instinct for it, in conflict with an inherited tradition that gives it no encouragement. Blake, although he definitely helped the Romantic Revival on its way, was himself, like Landor, rather an isolated manifestation of poetry belonging not very clearly to any particular age. The Romantic Revival, when it did come, came with a full force of reaction against the age of reason, with its often admirable rhetoric, its emotional timidity and its concern with etiquette at the expense of character. But the Romantic Revival, for all the splendour of its common spirit and the great personal genius of its masters, had one radical condition of weakness, namely, that it was a revival. In many ways it was, and remains, the richest period in English poetry, but it was also the first period in English poetry that had something in the inspiration of its actual poetic method that was second-hand and not original. This is not to say that Wordsworth and the others were not original poets. The discovery of nature, the revolutionary passion, the preoccupation with the everyday life of the emotions, one or another of these marked Keats and Shelley and Byron, and the rest of them, as discoverers. But in the actual machinery through which their poetic mood worked there was often something literary and remembered in a sense more marked than can be observed in the practice of poets in England before. It is true that no good poet has ever worked without some example in his mind, but the Elizabethans were conscious of an Italian influence as of something vivid and present among them, a very part of their own lives, as it were, whereas the Elizabethan influence upon Keats was something deliberately remembered, something won back from a long past age. Without in the least detracting from the achievement of Keats, which must remain among the greatest in English poetry, it may be said that in this respect the Elizabethans were Italians but that Keats imitated the Elizabethans. The poets of the Romantic Revival were as rich in creative endowment as the Elizabethans themselves, certainly richer than the Augustans. But, in a sense, even the polished formality of Pope's verse and the artificiality of his manner were more exactly his own than were the free music and luxurious emotional life the unaided discoveries of the Romantics who used them in the next age.

This circumstance of the Romantic Revival has had a profound influence upon English poetry ever since, and so far as may be prophesied it is likely to continue to do so. Poetry since the death of Keats and Shelley and Byron has acquired many new interests, chiefly intellectual interests, which did not belong to it before their time, or, at least, did not belong to it in anything like the same measure, but it has, also, become definitely a less original thing both as to manner and in its emotional content. Whether this is a gain or loss is for each reader to determine for himself, but in the conclusion it is likely that there would be at least as many people glad of the fact as sorry for it. I must elaborate this position first as to the manner, and later as to the content.

I would be dogmatic at once and say that in spite of all the experimenters in *vers libre* and polyphonic prose and what not, there is now no new verse form to be discovered in English. Every poet as he comes along can invent new combinations of existing forms, often enchantingly, but that is another matter, though even this becomes increasingly difficult. Poetry will never take kindly to free verse as

B

a common method, though any poet is likely to practise it at intervals. So-called polyphonic prose, which is only a variety of free verse, may lend itself often to admirable writing when it happens to be used by an admirable writer, but for most of us it is incapable of the peculiar delight given by regular verse forms which have been evolved through centuries of experience. The introduction of classical metres into English poetry is a lost cause, as it always has been, attractive though it may be to a fine spirit now and again. There remains for the use of the poets the vast technique of recognised verse form with its infinite variety of line length and stanzaic structure. None of the considerable poets in our literature has ever found it irksome to work within these limitations, an observation which is as just to-day as it ever was. Since the Romantic poets the possibilities of line and stanza in themselves have hardly been extended in any important manner, unless we allow to the contrary, for example, Swinburne's exploitation of anapæstic measures, which, on the whole, was to the bad rather than to the good in spite of its occasional triumphs. Strictly speaking, as to line and stanza in themselves, it might be said that even the Romantics did nothing that could not be matched somewhere or another in English poetry before them. Their technical invention was mostly rediscovery, though none the less creditable to them for that. Their rediscovery was of something so forgotten that they might claim that it was new, but, however that may be, there has been nothing new since them in the strictly formal contour of English verse. What has been new, and what must always be new when a true poet is at work, is the rhythmic beat within that contour, and the genius of our language is happily such as to give this beat boundless freedom. Among our contemporaries no-one has achieved a technique more distinctively his own, perhaps, than Mr. Walter de la Mare, but upon examination it will be found that this distinctiveness is entirely one of this rhythmic beat, and that there is no invention of metrical form.

> " Is there anybody there ? " said the Traveller,
> Knocking on the moonlit door;

is peculiarly marked by Mr. de la Mare's rhythmic genius; but alter the beat a little and you get—

> And they changed their lives and departed, and
> came back as the leaves of the trees.

And again, to go back beyond Morris, we come even to—

> What are the wild waves saying,
> Sister, the whole day long?

Leaving out of the question the stanzaic form and line length, and the way these are set out on the printed page, there is in these three examples an almost exact stress-equivalence, but each has its own entirely individual rhythmic life; rather commonplace and obvious in the last of the three, deep-lunged and heroic in Morris, and very delicate and subtle in Mr. de la Mare.

It is true that now and again a poet even to-day may contrive charming variations upon stanzaic form, as Tennyson did in his *Recollections of the Arabian Nights*, or as Mr. Thomas Hardy has done more recently in many of his lyrics. Every now and again also a poet may invent some attractive little device of his own in the smaller things of technique, as, for example, Mr. Frank Kendon, a new poet who makes an interesting experiment with rhyme-sounds thus—musing, mind, attuned, despising. But there is no peculiar virtue in these gestures once their novelty has passed, and the fact remains that from the coming of Wordsworth until all our best contemporary poets, by far the greater part of the most original work, and important work, has been done in recognised verse forms, and it has relied for its personal accent upon an individual rhythmic beat within those forms. The domination of the rhymed heroic couplet in the age preceding Wordsworth was so complete as to make the return to other more definitely lyric measures almost a feat of invention, but, even so, it is doubtful whether there is any verse form used by Wordsworth or Blake or Shelley or Keats, or any of their contemporaries, which could not in its essential character be matched somewhere in the sixteenth or seventeenth centuries.

In its structural foundations, therefore, Victorian verse in England may be said to be a direct inheritance from the Romantic age, and through it from the longer general ancestry of English poetry. The body of fine work done between Victoria's succession and the death of Tennyson is sufficient proof that the poetic instinct of the race knew very well what it was about in this. At the same time, the more restless talents were sometimes troubled by allegiance to forms that, whatever their virtue, had no longer the first flush of inventive delight. The sombre, charnel-house genius of a Webster, the rugged,

almost fierce, intellectual power of a Ben
Jonson, the religious ecstasy of a Vaughan,
the tender irresponsibility of a Lovelace or
a Suckling, and the spiritual ingenuity of a
Donne, were all alike content to work in the
simplest lyric forms, and were able to find
complete expression through these, because
as forms they were still fresh enough to be for
each man treasure-trove. Nowhere in the
whole range of passion and wit and subtle
argument was there a mood to be found that
wanted at any time to break the mould. To
a large extent this has remained true until
our own day, but as time has gone on a poet
has now and again suddenly, as it were, become
too conscious of the long service already done
by the more established measures and has been
tempted into irregularities which have sometimes been admirable in result and have sometimes tumbled over into excesses only to be
forgotten. A great deal of Browning's verse
is the result of some such uneasiness in his
mind, a fear lest he should accept tradition
too easily, a deliberate realisation on his part
that a poet has to be original. Browning's
genius could stand the strain, but a strain
it was. Matthew Arnold's experiments in
free verse have much the same origin. He,
again, justified himself, but without doing

anything to show that the main traditions in which he worked habitually were becoming less important to English poetry. In the case of Whitman, the one example in the Victorian age of a great poetic genius working consistently without respect for the established practice of English verse, there is no doubt that to minds and ears aware of all that custom has achieved, a great energy denied itself more than half its effect.

Whitman's revolt was complete, and, broadly speaking, it has had no effect upon English poetry. Arnold's departures from established practice were occasional and, even so, pretty much in the example of Milton, who himself made but few experiments, and those not violent departures from the establishment. Browning's nonconformity was another matter. Unlike Whitman, he remained essentially always within the tradition, but his unrest within the tradition was more or less constant and not, as with Arnold, the accident of a mood here and there. Browning's was the most important poetic revolt of his age, and it is a revolt that is a matter of diction more precisely than of metrical form. And in its manner, as distinguished from its content, it is in diction that the Victorian age most importantly modified tradition. Leaving Whitman out

of the question, the Victorian use of verse
was, as we have seen, with one or two insignificant exceptions, an acknowledgment of the
fitness of all that had been done by the age-
long instinct of the race. Nor, taking the
Victorian achievement as a whole, shall we
find any violent or general change in the
management of diction itself. But practice
here was to some extent modified, and chiefly
by Browning and through his influence.

The history of diction in English poetry is
one that has never been written, and one that
would need a great volume of argument and
illustration. But taking a summary view
of the whole field certain characteristics define
themselves from age to age. The first generalisation that may be made about good diction
in poetry is that it should derive from the
common speech of the time and yet be a heightened idiomatic form of that speech, achieving
from the emotional pressure of poetry a new
dignity and beauty. And we shall find that
in English poetry the diction has always
associated itself in this way with the natural
speech of the time. Chaucer, in taking English
speech, and for the first time making it the
language of English literature, was dealing,
so far as we can reconstruct the facts of that
far-off time, with a language unsophisticated,

unlearned, and quite ingenuous in its sincerity.
And the language of his poetry is marked by
these qualities, quickened by the breath of
the poet's genius.

> Whan that Aprille with his shoures sote
> The droghte of Marche hath perced to the rote,
> And bathed every veyne in swich licour,
> Of which vertu engendred is the flour;
> Whan Zephirus eek with his swete breeth
> Inspired hath in every holt and heeth
> The tendre croppes, and the yonge sonne
> Hath in the Ram his halfe cours y-ronne,
> And smale fowle maken melodye,
> That slepen al the night with open yë,
> (So priketh hem nature in hir corages) :
> Than longen folk to goon on pilgrimages. . . .

Nothing could be simpler in the most literal
sense than the wording of this passage. It is
not the simplicity used by great genius to
enforce some tragic or tender crisis, but the
simplicity of a man who wants to make an
entirely matter-of-fact statement, but to make
it with dignity and authority. It is not
likely that the people of Chaucer's time talked
exactly like that, but it is certain that almost
any of them would understand what Chaucer
was saying without the smallest difficulty.
And we imagine that this clarity of statement
was, in fact, the chief idiomatic characteristic
of the common speech of the time, and that

Chaucer was, in diction, definitely the poet of his age in realising this. To read this opening of *The Canterbury Tales* over three or four times is to be struck more and more by the remarkable purity of the diction, and it may be said of Chaucer's work as a whole that the chief triumph of his dealing with language was that he took the simplicity which was common around him and transfigured it into that finer essence of simplicity which is purity. When two hundred years after Chaucer's death the great Elizabethans were in full song, much in the meantime had happened to common English. It had become instructed, more flexible in its intellectual play, richer in association, and rather more conscious of its own capacities. At the same time it was now the instrument of a people fired with ardent enthusiasm, rich in enterprise, and glowing with the vitality of a young and prospering national spirit. It was the speech of witty, passionate, and powerful youth, and triumphant youth, delighting in problems both of body and mind, immensely fertile in its resources. But it had not yet become sophisticated, and that is the great bond between it and the speech of Chaucer's time, and the great difference between it and the speech of later ages. And, again, these characteristics which we suppose with good reason to have been those of everyday speech are to be found completely explored and enriched in the age's poetry. And one of Shakespeare's sonnets may stand in witness of what was within the common practice of the poets of the age.

But wherefore do not you a mightier waie
Make warre vppon this bloudie tirant time?
And fortifie your selfe in your decay
With meanes more blessed then my barren rime?
Now stand you on the top of happie houres,
And many maiden gardens, yet vnset,
With vertuous wish would beare your liuing flowers,
Much liker then your painted counterfeit:
So should the lines of life that life repaire
Which this (Time's pensel or my pupill pen)
Neither in inward worth nor outward faire
Can make you liue your selfe in eies of men,
   To giue away your selfe, keeps your selfe still,
   And you must liue drawne by your owne sweet skill.

In the succeeding age, from the Elizabethans to the Augustans, the same principle may be discovered in the practice of poets as different in their personal quality as, say, Donne, Milton and Lovelace. Donne's—

By Absence this good means I gain
   That I can catch her
   Where none can watch her,
In some close corner of my brain:
   There I embrace and kiss her
   And so enjoy her and none miss her . . .

may have perplexed his readers by its intellectual turn, but it cannot have seemed anything
but easily natural to them in its actual word.
If Donne was startling, it was in what he said
and not at all in his way of saying it. And
so with Milton. Common speech could never
put on a sublimer transfiguration than in such
passages as—

> Weep no more, woful Shepherds, weep no more,
> For Lycidas your sorrow is not dead,
> Sunk though he be beneath the watry floar,
> So sinks the day-star in the ocean bed,
> And yet anon repairs his drooping head,
> And tricks his beams, and with new-spangled Ore
> Flames in the forehead of the morning sky. . . .

But it remains the common speech that is
being so dignified. Milton's diction, more
eminently poetical perhaps than any other
in the language, is still founded on the grave,
full-syllabled Biblical idiom that we are sure
was current in the ordinary enlightened speech
of the time. The first readers of his poems
would find a familiar tongue, however unsus-
pected was the beauty that it revealed to them.
And in the lighter lyrists of that age, this
relation of poetic to common speech, secured
without any apparent deliberation—we may
indeed say definitely without it—and yet

achieving the magic with easy certainty, shines round us on every hand.

> Tell me not, Sweet, I am unkind
>   That from the nunnery
> Of thy chaste breast and quiet mind
>   To war and arms I fly . . .

and—

> Shut not so soon; the dull-eyed night
>   Has not as yet begun
> To make a seizure on the light,
>   Or to seal up the sun . . .

and—

> Out upon it, I have loved
>   Three whole days together
> And am like to love three more
>   If it prove fair weather . . .

are all alike loyal both to poetry and to the common English of their time. Nor do the lyrists whose raptures were less of the world go elsewhere for their means of expression. Vaughan, with—

> Happy those early days, when I
> Shined in my Angel-infancy !
> Before I understood this place
> Appointed for my second race,
> Or taught my soul to fancy aught
> But a white, celestial thought. . . .

and Herbert with—

> Sweet day, so cool, so calm, so bright,
> The bridal of the earth and sky—
> The dew shall weep thy fall to-night
> For thou must die. . . .

and Crashaw with—

> Since 'tis not to be had at home
> She'll travel for a martyrdom. . . .

follow the same poetic instinct precisely.

When we pass into a world of new artistic aim, the world of which Alexander Pope is president, we find the same thing happening. The worldly pilgrims of Chaucer's book, Elizabeth's intrepid adventurers, the saintly learning and gestured gallantry that fought it out in Puritan England, have in turn passed from the centre of the stage of articulate national life, to make way for the man about town, the philanderer, the coquette, and the sententious moralist. The innuendo and the moral precept are together on every man's lips, not wholly insincere in their partnership. And the idiom of this witty, argumentative, intriguing and rather self-righteous society is perfectly turned to the uses of genius in the Popean poetry. When *The Dunciad* and *The Essay on Man* and the *Epistle to Dr. Arbuthnot* were first read, the coffee-houses and boudoirs may have been moved by every varying degree of delight and resentment, but nobody questioned that here was the common language and that at the same time it was being used above the common pitch. Pastoral, invective, worldly-wisdom, religious philosophising, the same instrument was there exactly tempered for each alike, thus—

> Whose herds with milk, whose fields with bread,
> Whose flocks supply him with attire;
> Whose trees in summer yield him shade,
>   In winter fire.

and—

> One dedicates in high heroic prose,
> And ridicules beyond a hundred foes :
> One from all Grub Street will my fame defend,
> And, more abusive, calls himself my friend.
> This prints my letters, that expects a bribe,
> And others roar aloud, " Subscribe, subscribe ! " ...

and—

> A little learning is a dangerous thing,
> Drink deep, or taste not the Pierian spring . . .

and—

> All nature is but art unknown to thee,
> All chance, direction which thou can'st not see;
> All discord, harmony not understood :
> All partial evil, universal good ;
> And, spite of pride, in erring reason's spite,
> One truth is clear, Whatever is, is right.

It is true that the Augustan school in its
decline, which was contemporary with the
faint prelude of the Romantic Revival, fell
into an extreme artificiality of diction that
can hardly have had its model even by suggestion in the common speech of the time.
So good a poet as Gray, who was himself
one of the preludists, was not blameless in
this respect, and could write—

> Him the dog of darkness spied,
> His shaggy throat he open'd wide,
> While from his jaws, with carnage fill'd,
> Foam and human gore distill'd :
> Hoarse he bays with hideous din,
> Eyes that glow, and fangs that grin ;
> And long pursues, with fruitless yell,
> The father of the powerful spell . . .

which Collins, at his best even surer than Gray
in prophecy of a new age, could match with—

> Whilst Vengeance, in the lurid air,
> Lifts her red arm, exposed and bare :
> On whom that ravening brood of Fate,
> Who lap the blood of sorrow, wait :
> Who, Fear, this ghastly train can see,
> And look not madly wild, like thee ?

These excesses were, however, at no time
characteristic of the better poets of the time,
and were rather the mumbo-jumbo of versifiers
who, lacking any personal inspiration, caught a

rumour at second or even third hand of a spurious Arcadia, and rhymed it—or blank-versed it—into a spiritless rhetoric. It is only suggestive at a very distant cry, and by the merest implication, of the true nature of Augustan poetry that Richard Jago could write—

> And oft the stately Tow'rs, that overtop
> The rising Wood, and oft the broken Arch,
> Or mould'ring Wall, well taught to counterfeit
> The Waste of Time, to solemn Thought excite,
> And crown with graceful Pomp the shaggy Hill.

No age of English poetry has suffered more in reputation through the malpractices of its more undistinguished writers than that of Pope, and in all its finer expression it worked its own way as closely in touch as any other with the ordinary speech of its own time.

In these references to common speech, the standard referred to, it may be said, is the speech of the intelligent and vivid, though not necessarily the most highly educated, members of the community. There is no telling at any time where exactly you are going to catch the true turn of racy or imaginative idiom, and it is as unsafe to generalise in favour of the rustic as it is to do so in favour of the tutored townsman. Good minds make good speech, and cumulatively they give the common

C

diction of an age a character which cannot escape the poets when poetry has any health in it, which, to do it justice in looking back over five hundred years of achievement, is nearly always. Apart from those lapses of quite unrepresentative poets, the relation which is being discussed was preserved, as we have seen, with unbroken continuity from the beginnings down to the time of the late Augustans, the immediate predecessors of Wordsworth.

While, however, the poetasters of the Popean descent * are now seen clearly enough to have fallen far short of the poetic stature of their time, they were widely read and admired, and in 1798, when Wordsworth prefaced the *Lyrical Ballads* with the now famous but then slightly noted challenge to a false poetic diction, their example seemed no doubt to be a more dangerous influence than was in fact the case. If Wordsworth's protest had never been explicitly made, we should have lost a

---

* The sifting of the minor poetic writers of the eighteenth century is a task to which critical attention is now being very profitably turned. Many readers of poetry no doubt associate Richard Jago and Matthew Green, for example, in their minds as belonging to the same negligible group, whereas Jago was a poor dull fellow in verse and Green a very considerable poet indeed.

masterpiece of critical prose, but English
poetry would none the less surely have remained
loyal to the principle that Wordsworth so
earnestly advocated. The big men had never
lost sight of it, nor were they in any general
sense likely to. In attacking the windy
pomposity that for a time stole poetic honours,
with a power that flattered its importance,
Wordsworth did not recognise that, among
the more considerable poets, even those who
were demonstrably touched by the falsity of
style prevalent among their inferiors were
at the same time preparing the reform of which
he himself was the new and conscious gospeller.
Gray who, as has been shown, could belabour
his muse with any of them, and who was named
by Wordsworth as a particular example for
censure, did also write the *Elegy*, in which
whatever lapses there may be are far more
than atoned for in the main movement by the
very purity of style which was the aim of
Wordsworth's pleading. Wordsworth's cause
was a just one, but it was also one that was
obvious to the genius of English poetry, and
the fact that he was as consciously preoccupied
with it as he was is not without its reflection
in his own creative work. He was sometimes
ridden by his theory, and then the lovely
simplicity that was the basis of a style that is

at the height of English poetry lopped over into mere banality. But in his normal manner Wordsworth exemplified his critical position with complete success, and nowhere more strikingly than in his most inspired passages. The spoken English with which his creative mood was familiar must have been a blend drawn from the serious intellectualism of young literary society, the forthright simplicities of the northern dalesmen, where an old Biblical tradition coloured a natural austerity, with touches of paternal authority and undergraduate levity—or perhaps a little less than levity. It was the speech of a new England, sophisticated, politically self-conscious, rather heavily dialectical, but it was saved by the Bible, the dalesman, and a community of wit. It was such a speech, played upon by that knowledge of the poet's literary ancestry which is a necessary agent always in the transmutation, that Wordsworth subdued exactly to his imaginative purposes.

> Will no one tell me what she sings?
>   Perhaps the plaintive numbers flow
> For old, unhappy, far-off things,
>   And battles long ago:
> Or is it some more humble lay,
> Familiar matter of to-day?
> Some natural sorrow, loss, or pain,
> That has been, and may be again!

Wordsworth's great contemporaries, each in his own way, in terms of his own temperament, were guided by the same principle. The whole nature of Burns's genius was governed by his will to sing the common speech of Scotland into immortality. The *beau monde*, the gaming rooms and the prize-ring, the purlieus of scandal and the solitudes of romantic exile filled with the whispers of poetry and heroic history, the world of new loves and lost causes, of literary loyalties and animosities, among which Byron moved indifferently, in or out of temper, all spoke their own language in the motley of his verse. To know the poet and his environment is to see the same essential man in—

Smart uniforms and sparkling coronets
　　Are spurned in turn, until her turn arrives,
After male loss of time, and hearts, and bets
　　Upon the sweepstakes for substantial wives;
And when at last the pretty creature gets
　　Some gentleman, who fights, or writes, or drives,
It soothes the awkward squad of the rejected
To find how very badly she selected . . .

and in—

The mountains look on Marathon—
　　And Marathon looks on the sea;
And musing there an hour alone,
　　I dreamed that Greece might still be free;
For standing on the Persians' grave,
I could not deem myself a slave.

Even Shelley, or that mood in him that was preoccupied with the fiery pinnacles in the clouds, kept the diction of his most ethereal flights in tune with the same instinctive necessity.

> The glory of her being, issuing thence,
> Stains the dead, blank, cold air, with a warm shade
> Of unentangled intermixture, made
> By Love, of light and motion : one intense
> Diffusion, one serene Omnipresence,
> Whose flowing outlines mingle in their flowing,
> Around her cheeks and utmost fingers glowing
> With the unintermitted blood, which there
> Quivers (as in a fleece of snow-like air
> The crimson pulse of living morning quiver).
> Continuously prolonged, and ending never,
> Till they are lost, and in that Beauty furled
> Which penetrates and clasps and fills the world;
> Scarce visible from extreme loveliness . . .

may perhaps at first glance be elusive in its precise meaning, but it is not because of anything difficult or uncommon in the actual words, but because the poet's mind is engaged with an almost indefinable emotion. Keats again, for all the emphasis of a clear literary influence upon his diction, was never anything but easily intelligible in his actual statement to the simplest reader. *The Eve of St. Agnes* and *Isabella*, even the odes, might have come out a little differently if there had been no

Spenser or Marlowe or Chapman, but the reader
of 1820 had no need to be a scholar of Elizabethan poetry to perceive every shade of their
beauty as they were. Alone among the great
poets of his time, Coleridge at intervals sounded
tones in his verse that were archaic, or purely
fanciful rather, not recognisably out of the
English of daily use.

> He holds him with his skinny hand,
> " There was a ship," quoth he.
> " Hold off ! unhand me, grey-beard loon ! "
> Eftsoons his hand dropt he.

Coming upon that at the opening of *The Ancient
Mariner*, the first readers of *Lyrical Ballads*
must have been conscious that something
a little odd was here being done with language.
But such things are incidents merely even in
Coleridge's style, and need not be stressed.
In any case they were, it may be, done more
than half humorously, and for the most part
Coleridge—in the work of his that matters—
was as sure as Wordsworth himself in the purity
of his diction, in drawing it from the one
wholesome source.

> Therefore all seasons shall be sweet to thee,
> Whether the summer clothe the general earth
> With greenness, or the redbreast sit and sing
> Betwixt the tufts of snow on the bare branch
> Of mossy apple-tree, while the high thatch

Smokes in the sun-thaw; whether the eave-drops fall
Heard only in the trances of the blast,
Or if the secret ministry of frost
Shall hang them up in silent icicles,
Quietly shining to the quiet moon.

Beside which may be set, as a final example
from that age of what poetry can do in the way
of transfiguring plain speech, Landor's—

> Stand close around, ye Stygian set,
>   With Dirce in one boat convey'd !
> Or Charon, seeing, may forget
>   That he is old and she a shade.

III

By the time the Victorian masters were
beginning to write, the English language, in
the common use of it, had thus gone through
many adventures. Shaping itself to the
typical or representative national temper
and aspirations from one age to another,
it had been dominantly in succession naïf,
lusty, sacramental, witty and didactic, high-
flown in its excesses, and then learned and
argumentative with a leaven of yeoman cor-
rection in it under Wordsworth's control.
These characteristics had in turn passed into
the texture of English poetry, and each had
left something of its mark upon the future

practice of the art, complicating it and making it more and more subject to a conscious literary deliberation. And now the example of Byron, with his cosmopolitan and sometimes journalistic use of language, of Keats with his intense brooding upon and requickening of an antique mode, of Shelley with his almost fanatical demands upon the spiritual resources of words, had further extended the range of poetic diction and at the same time increased the difficulties in the way of original mastery. These problems may seem to be artificial as here stated, and in a sense they are so. Poetry is neither more nor less difficult at one time than another, given the poet. But in the light of achievement we may not unprofitably consider what are the conditions that have governed that achievement from age to age, and so perhaps at least correct some of the false and easy notions that we are apt to foster about the art of our own time, when we approach it unset in its right historical perspective. Tennyson and Browning and Arnold and the Rossettis and Morris and Swinburne give us the delight of experience perfectly expressed, and that is the first, and in a way the last, thing to be said about them as poets. But, coming when they did, they were confronted with special problems in the practice of their art, and we lose nothing of our enjoyment of their essential poetry in understanding what those problems were.

English poetry was now nearly five hundred years old. In its creation immense demands had been made upon the language, and many characteristic beauties of poetic style might well have been supposed to have been now explored beyond further possibilities. When Chaucer wrote, the inspiration as of divinely wise and happy childhood could shine through the most ingenuous of phrases, and the plainest statement was touched by magic for ever in this playground of poetry's infancy. " O yonge fresshe folkes," he exclaims, or " Now shippes sailinge in the sea," or " A nightingale, upon a cedre grene," or " Ther sprang the violete all newe," and we have with every word the enchanted discovery of poetry. Thereafter a poet might score a great effect now and again by placing some such utter simplicity in the midst of subtler or more elaborate state-ment, but it could hardly again be used as a customary manner. What was then and has ever since remained triumphantly original in Chaucer could but become commonplace on repetition. His way of saying delightedly that the flowers were fresh and the birds were glad and that apples were sweet, and saying

these things just as simply as that, stands
beside his humorous invention of character
as one of the two chief glories of his poetry,
but it was not a case of his faintly suggesting
a poetic possibility that could be elaborated
by his successors. He took the obvious and
without embroidering it with a single word
made it into poetry of everlasting freshness,
but he did this once and for all, and poets
after him would have to add some touch of
revelation of their own before they could make
good their claim. Chaucer could say that
flowers were fresh and leave it at that, giving
us a perfect image of spring, but even two
hundred years later, in what now seems to us
to have been still the dawn of English poetry,
Shakespeare had to make his impression with
a far more complex image—

> daffodils,
> That come before the swallow dares, and take
> The winds of March with beauty.

By the time that Tennyson began to write,
Shakespeare's necessity was even plainer.
The thousand simple circumstances of nature
and humanity were still an inevitable part of
the poet's content matter. In the course of
a lifework of artistic creation he could not but
want to say a dozen times that the grass was
green and the sky blue, the water clear and

love uncertain, and it is merely pointless to
forbid him these things because they have been
said before. But apart from that allowance
of an occasional *cliché*, admitted because of
some virtue as contrast, as for example when
Tennyson says—

> On one side lay the ocean, and on one
> Lay a great water, and the moon was full . . .

he had to say these things with just as much
originality of phrase as would compel attention,
and yet with not one word beyond this, or one
word too heavily weighted, lest he should be
accused of inflation, which is the death of poetry.

A second difficulty that Tennyson, to use the
one example for the moment, had to meet was
in connection with the associative value of
words. When Chaucer was writing, words
can have had little or no associative value.*
Even with Shakespeare they must have had
far less of this evocative power than they had
three hundred years later. Indeed, Shakespeare's own language has unquestionably
for us acquired a certain patina from time.
We read to-day—

> When to the sessions of sweet silent thought,

---

* That is to say, Chaucer's language as intelligible
to us. Lost in it, no doubt, are associations from
earlier speech.

and upon analysis we are aware of two separate
sources of our delight in the superbly used word
" sessions." Firstly, there is its purely imaginative value. For Shakespeare, " sessions " can
have had but one literal meaning. In the
framing of that line the common marvel of
creative imagination was performed. The poet
deliberated upon his thoughts gathering together
for the survey of " things past." It was a
process something formal and ceremonious that
he had in mind, a solemn conclave. Thus the
ritual of the law would suggest itself to him,
the ordered gravity of a court, the pregnant
occasion of a sessions. And thereupon the two
ideas would associate themselves, the perfect
image would be created, and with it would come
the full exercise of our imaginative powers in
turn, of our best delight in poetry. For the
bare actual setting of the scene in his sonnet
Shakespeare might have been content with
some such line as—

When to my mind I summon up things past,

but the informing vitality would have escaped.
It is one of the mysteries of poetry that when
you translate her word into another, although
by logic it may seem to be the same thing, it
is in truth something essentially different.
It is not quite a barren truism to say that you

can only say what Shakespeare said by saying
what he said—

> When to the sessions of sweet silent thought
> I summon up remembrance of things past.

This, then, is the first value that we discover in
Shakespeare's use in that connection of the
word " sessions "—an exact functioning of
the poetic imagination. But over and above
that there is yet another value, one that is not
very easy to define in set terms, and one of
which Shakespeare himself can hardly have
been consciously aware. " Sessions," as we now
read the word, calls to our mind, as it did to
his, a court of law with all its weighty circumstance; also, as we read it in the sonnet, we
get precisely the effect of pure imaginative
effort that Shakespeare got, or as much of it
as is possible to our own faculty; but the word
has also taken on a strange atmospheric significance, almost a shade of actual meaning that
is beyond its original intention. In its strictly
imaginative value alone, the word was one that
might without offence have been more or less
similarly used by one of Shakespeare's contemporaries or early successors, even after his
brilliant discovery of it in that context. Shakespeare's choice of the word was entirely
admirable for his imaginative purpose, but it

was not so astonishing as to make it explicitly
his own beyond the use of any other poet who
wished to escape the charge of mere theft.
But as time went on, the word, fixed there in
its sonnet, underwent a spiritual evolution, that
for practical purposes was complete in any case
by the time Tennyson arrived, until it was in
some sense of a newly acquired nature, and no
longer safe for any poet's handling. The word
could not now be used in anything approach-
ing the same context without calling up in the
reader's mind the whole dark and passionate
background of Shakespeare's sonnets. It has,
in short, acquired a specifically literary association, which is to say—although some critics
would seem to overlook the fact—that it is the
living witness of one of the supreme moments
of human experience, but also that it has become
so essential a part of that particular moment
that it is now almost impossible to use it in
the service of any other. And when Tennyson
began to write he found a language that was
strewn with words that had put on this dangerous nature, beautiful and often as it would
appear irreplaceable words, yet now with
calamity in their touch for the poet. To
reject them was by no means the same thing as
rejecting the false " poetic " inflation that had
been the mark of Wordsworth's attack. It

meant that by now a new discipline of a very arduous and vigilant kind had become necessary in the practice of poetry. On every hand were admirable and seductive instruments the use of which was forbidden. If you were Keats you might privateer among the old poetry with profit, but his success in this matter was the adventure of lucky genius, not an example to be followed. Shakespeare could write

> Not poppy nor mandragora
> Nor all the drowsy syrups of this world . . .

and Keats could find his Autumn sleeping

> Drowsed with the fume of poppies . . .

and be justified of his borrowing, but the exile from poetry of " drowsing " and " poppies " in company, which had at least been suggested by Shakespeare's lines, was now in any case absolute. So that the poet's craft is already complicated in two ways. If Tennyson in his verse wanted to recall the birds in spring, he could no longer rely for his effect upon some simple statement such as " the happy birds sang on the bough," and, further, in his elaborated image he had studiously to keep clear, for example, of

> Bare ruined choirs where late the sweet birds sang—

although the chances were that this superb and complex image would be insinuatingly persistent in his mind.

But these were not the only difficulties to be met in the management of diction. I have referred to Byron's occasional " journalistic use of language." Every now and again someone raises a false issue as between journalism and literature, suggesting that literature is arrogant in looking upon journalism as being less exalted than itself. It is the same kind of silly baiting as is sometimes indulged in between actors and dramatists, when it is indignantly suggested that it is an affront to the admirable art of Burbage to hold that it is, if the comparison must be made, on a lower creative plane than that of Shakespeare. Journalism, decently practised, can be as honourable and useful a profession as any other, and one to show natural gifts of taste and presentation to great advantage. But journalism is not literature, nor are its aims or methods those of literature. That literature often appears in the journals is beside the point. The essential condition of journalism is that it seeks either to report a fact or an event in terms that shall be immediately intelligible to the great mass of people, or to reflect an opinion from that mass in equally intelligible terms for the satisfaction

D

of the individual units that make up that mass.
Its business particularly is to accept and to
report, and when it uses invention—which it
must be allowed it often does—it is always
invention of the wrong kind.   To literature, on
the other hand, fact and event mean nothing
until they are related to an idea, or are seen in
conjunction with character, or found to be
useful for illuminating the experience of a
particular temperament, and further, in precise
contrast to journalism, literature seeks to
reflect an individual opinion for the benefit or
pleasure of the mass so far as the mass cares to
take any notice of it.   Thus " James Jones, a
casual labourer, was yesterday convicted at
the Clerkenwell Sessions of stealing a cigarette
box, the property of Mr. Thomas Jackson, M.P.,
and was sentenced to one month's hard labour "
is journalism, while Mr. Galsworthy's *Silver
Box* is literature.   Again, " To-day we celebrate
the tercentenary of the death of one of the
greatest of all Englishmen.   We have sometimes
been called a nation of shopkeepers, and yet
no country is richer in her poets than England,
and of these the acknowledged chief is William
Shakespeare.   Here was one who sounded the
full gamut of human passions, and the univer-
sality of his genius has carried his fame into
every quarter of the civilized globe.   We

honour not only Shakespeare, but ourselves in drinking to-day to the immortal memory of one whose work will endure as long as the English language is spoken "—is an example of journalism at its idlest, while Ben Jonson's panegyric and Arnold's sonnet, separated by two hundred and fifty years, are alike literature.

The flood of this journalism, considerable in Tennyson's time and almost devastating in our own, has added seriously to the poet's difficulties in the use of language. Whole tracts of English have been turned over to the service of this business of conveying useless information to people who are no whit the better for receiving it, or of giving an appearance of independent profundity to rough and ready mass opinion. The language has in consequence become so infested with *clichés* that a whole school of writers has arisen whose sole ambition would seem to be an ostentatious avoidance of these. Byron, the first great English poet to allow a humorous-ironic strain to run through the body of his serious poetry, as apart from professed satire, frequently made effective use of this journalistic quality in language, and the practice has been a common one with explicitly comic writers in verse ever since. But in doing this Byron exploited the growing activities of the Press very happily to his own purposes, without in any way enlarging the range of expression for poetry's normal habit. The success of his licence, indeed, made the conditions of diction even more exacting for his successors, since the journalistic *cliché* once dignified by literary usage was more definitely than ever ruled out as a poetic instrument. Fortune had rewarded the brave once, but the second comer could only expect to be dubbed foolhardy. After Byron, poetry had to remind herself that to relate her diction to the common idiomatic speech of her time and to relate it to the sophisticated periods of the leading article or the heavy facetiousness of the debating room were quite different things. She had to be careful not to be beguiled into doing seriously what Byron had done brilliantly with his tongue in his cheek. She had brought off a very good joke out of motley once, but that was enough; henceforth it must be played, when at all, in full livery with cap and bells complete. The improviser had for once become the seer by some caprice of inspiration, and poetry would be wise to leave it at that.*

Finally, Tennyson found a language that as a literary vehicle was nearly five hundred years old, three hundred at least of which had

---

* These remarks, it need hardly be added, apply to part of Byron's work only.

been of rich and unceasing activity. This fact presented a difficulty distinct from that which has been examined in connection with Shakespeare's use of the word "sessions." Not only had particular words acquired a specific associative value which made them dangerous for use again in poetry, but the whole construction of a poetic phrase was now beset by mazes of seductive suggestion, word calling up word in long sequence from the vast stores of poetry, that had been accumulated by the race. It was no longer a very easy thing to see the object before you, precisely in its immediate appearance, wholly dissociated from any company that it might have kept in some earlier creative presentation. It needed something of a conscious effort in looking at yellow sands to remind yourself that coral was not necessarily somewhere about, to remember that an albatross was not positively doomed to meet its death from a cross-bow, to hear the nightingale without hearing also the undertones of "tears amid the alien corn," to see a country graveyard wholly unshadowed by the ghosts of village Hampdens and mute inglorious Miltons. There was no simple way of escape for the poet from this storied experience of his ancestry. He had to face it courageously like the rest of experience, to assimilate and master it, and in so far as it passed into his work at all, as it was bound to do in some measure, to stamp it with his own pressure and so recreate it. But it did complicate his task. We may now see how Tennyson dealt with this and the other problems that have been presented.

IV

In connection with his diction it will be convenient at first to consider a single poem of Tennyson's, which embodies most of the characteristics of his style—this from *In Memoriam*—

> Calm is the morn without a sound,
>   Calm as to suit a calmer grief,
>   And only thro' the faded leaf
> The chestnut pattering to the ground :
>
> Calm and deep peace on this high wold,
>   And on these dews that drench the furze,
>   And all the silvery gossamers
> That twinkle into green and gold :
>
> Calm and still light on yon great plain
>   That sweeps with all its autumn bowers,
>   And crowded farms and lessening towers,
> To mingle with the bounding main :
>
> Calm and deep peace in this wide air,
>   These leaves that redden to the fall;
>   And in my heart, if calm at all,
> If any calm, a calm despair :

Calm on the seas, and silver sleep,
  And waves that sway themselves in rest,
  And dead calm in that noble breast
Which heaves but with the heaving deep.

First in these lines is apparent a poetic virtue of which Tennyson was an almost constant master, the faculty for seeing a natural object in minutely exact definition. " Thro' the faded leaf The chestnut pattering to the ground," the " dews that drench the furze," the whole of the third stanza, the " waves that sway themselves in rest," each phrase is incontrovertible evidence of a thing personally seen with creative intensity. In the first of these examples we see how Tennyson could manage that elaboration of the simple statement, which is the first of the four problems that have been discussed as awaiting him. If Chaucer had been presenting an autumn landscape—which, in his preoccupation with spring, he very rarely did— and had wanted to use foliage as a figure, he would almost certainly have been content with " the faded leaf " without embellishment, and from his tongue the economy would have been convincing. But by Tennyson's time the phrase by itself would have been something barren, and it needed fertilising by some further imaginative life. To the simple image Tennyson adds another, and together they brighten into one perfect realisation. Faded leaves, falling chestnuts—there for any schoolboy's observation, and yet, placed thus exactly, the witnesses of a rich poetic power in full exercise. And whenever Tennyson felt called upon to intensify the simple statement of a natural object, he was able to do it by reference to his own vivid experience, and thus to deal satisfactorily with the problem in question, and also, so far as the delineation of landscape (as apart from the further questions of human emotion and character) was concerned, to keep his yellow sands away from coral. If he wants to speak of marshy waste-lands, the "glooming flats" of Lincolnshire are to mind for his purpose, and the "glooming" is the signature written at once; if the violets were to blow, he had seen them "thick by ashen roots"; and even the familiar poppy in sleep he has seen precisely hanging from "the craggy ledge." I have said that Tennyson heightened his images in this way whenever he felt called upon to do so—called upon, that is to say, by the unaccountable poetic impulse. It was, even with so deliberate an artist, no matter of course to do this, and he was often, and by a just instinct, content to leave the simple image in its simplicity, though he would be careful not to leave it unfortified by some such intensi-

fication near at hand.   Love is to be looked for
not only " by the happy threshold," but also

> hand in hand with Plenty in the maize,
> Or red with spirted purple of the vats,
> Or foxlike in the vine . . .

though sometimes the poet leaves magic to
the barest statement with an entirely just
confidence, as in—

And the sun went down, and the stars came out far
over the summer sea . . .

where even Chaucer is matched for rich
economy of descriptive effect.   In which connection it may be as well here to remark that
Tennyson was a notable example of the poets
who pass in the evolution of their style from a
luxuriously decorative manner to this same
economy as a final characteristic.   And it is
a characteristic that can be arrived at through
evolution only, it can never as it were be
jumped at in the beginning.   The simplicity
of ignorance is inevitably bald commonplace,
but the simplicity slowly achieved out of a
vast poetic experience may be *Crossing the Bar*.
It may be worth while to look again at this
noble lyric, set beside something of the poet's
early luxuriance.   *The Lady of Shalott* was
written when he was twenty-three years old :—

A bow-shot from her bower-eaves,
He rode between the barley-sheaves,
The sun came dazzling thro' the leaves,
And flamed upon the brazen greaves
      Of bold Sir Lancelot.
A red-cross knight for ever kneel'd
To a lady in his shield,
That sparkled on the yellow field,
      Beside remote Shalott.

.   .   .   .

All in the blue unclouded weather
Thick-jewell'd shone the saddle-leather,
The helmet and the helmet-feather
Burn'd like one burning flame together,
      As he rode down to Camelot.
As often thro' the purple night,
Below the starry clusters bright,
Some bearded meteor, trailing light,
      Moves over still Shalott.

The missal-like illumination of verse such as
this will be further mentioned, but for the
moment I want merely to contrast it with this,
written sixty years later, when the poet was
over eighty :—

Sunset and evening star,
      And one clear call for me !
And may there be no moaning of the bar,
      When I put out to sea.

But such a tide as moving seems asleep,
      Too full for sound and foam,
When that which drew from out the boundless
      deep
      Turns again home.

Twilight and evening bell,
  And after that the dark !
And may there be no sadness of farewell,
  When I embark;

For tho' from out our bourne of Time and Place
  The flood may bear me far,
I hope to see my Pilot face to face
  When I have crost the bar.

In the diction of that there is a serene directness
that has been won only out of many years of
technical liberality.

The second of our problems in diction, that
of keeping clear of words with a too definitely
associative value, Tennyson met in his best
work by a steady concentration on his own
subject. Although in actual craftsmanship
he was sophisticated and selective in a far more
than common degree, an unusually self-
conscious artist, in the spiritual and emotional
content of his poetry Tennyson had hardly any
virtuosity at all. His success or failure in
philosophic originality will be discussed in a
later section of this essay, but the point here is
that in the experiences of his soul he may often
have been strangely disingenuous for a major
poet, but he was always absolutely himself.
His poetic technique is clearly and manifoldly
subject to influence—Shakespeare, Milton, Pope
even, Byron by glimpses, Keats—without any

one of these his manner would have been a little different, but upon the emotional life of his poetry there is practically no literary influence discernible at all. The tumultuous passion of the Elizabethans, the subtle lay metaphysic of Donne, Milton's darkly voluptuous Puritanism, Herrick's exquisitely tutored rustic urbanity, Wordsworth's moral clairvoyance—all these might never have existed in poetry at all for the traces of them to be found in the self-portraiture figured in Tennyson's art. Whether the fact is to be accounted as a defect or a virtue depends upon what we ask of poetry. To return to our passage from *In Memoriam*—

Calm is the morn without a sound . . .

we cannot but at once allow the obvious excellence of the mere writing, but if we want acute analysis of sorrow in her more elusive moods or discovering flights of mysticism, we shall find little enough of satisfaction. Here is nothing but the most childlike assertion of calm grief and its reflection in the calm dissolution of an autumn landscape. But if we are content with a mood so unvexed by argument, a thought so incapable of obscurity, we shall be well rewarded. For this very fixity of emotional purpose, to be confused perhaps by an unsympathetic judgment with an empty self-sufficiency, achieves its own purity of poetic style with, for us, its accompanying delight. It is just because Tennyson is so singly intent upon the elementary content matter of his poetry that he has no need of care to avoid assuming other men's emotions, or, more precisely, their emotional accent. In the " calm is the morn " passage there is not a word that is obviously reminiscent. Tennyson's mind may be a figure of homespun in the intellectual world, but it can appear in any company without the slightest embarrassment and apparently without any temptation to ape livelier or more ceremonious wits. This poet was in a literal sense too simple to be in even remote danger of borrowing " sessions."

Of the journalistic virus Tennyson's style cannot be said to be so entirely free. When he was concerned with the life of his own moods he was, as has just been said, proof against poetic suggestion from without, but when his subject was some public occasion or some external event that only accidentally came within his own experience, he was not so wholly proof against the *clichés* of journalism. It is true that he was one of the best occasional poets in the language, and particularly in the graver manner of his laureate office. And yet,

even in the justly famous *Ode on the Death of
the Duke of Wellington* there is, in parts at
least, a lower level of integrity in expression
than, for example again, in our passage from
In Memoriam, where, with the doubtful
exception of " that noble breast," there is not
a word that is not manifestly of the poet's
own minting. But in the Ode, written clearly
upon an occasion by which Tennyson was
deeply moved, and one rich in associations
that were of peculiar appeal to his genius, he
cannot keep his style wholly free of editorial
influence. This is not to speak in disparagement of a poem to which on the whole the term
magnificent is not misapplied, and one of the
supreme successes of its kind. But to acknowledge this is not to concede that the whole of
the splendid eulogy of " the statesman-warrior,
moderate, resolute " is couched in terms of
pure poetry. It was hardly the Tennyson of
the finest authority whom we find addressing
Nelson thus—

> Thine island loves thee well, thou famous man,
> The greatest sailor since our world began . . .

and Wellington as—

> England's greatest son,
> He that gain'd a hundred fights,
> Nor ever lost an English gun . . .

and as being
> as the greatest only are,
> In his simplicity sublime . . .

who called upon an unregenerate world to
> Let his great example stand
> Colossal, seen of every land . . .

and exclaimed that on Napoleon's overthrow
at Waterloo
> Heaven flash'd a sudden jubilant ray.

These are not the simplicities of
> Calm and deep peace in this wide air,
> These leaves that redden to the fall;
> And in my heart, if calm at all,
> If any calm, a calm despair . . .

nor of such things as this, from the Ode itself—
> More than is of man's degree
> Must be with us, watching here
> At this, our great solemnity.
> Whom we see not we revere,
> We revere, and we refrain
> From talk of battles loud and vain,
> And brawling memories all too free
> For such a wise humility
> As befits a solemn fane :
> We revere, and while we hear
> The tides of Music's golden sea
> Setting towards eternity,
> Uplifted high in heart and hope are we,
> Until we doubt not that for one so true
> There must be other nobler work to do
> Than when he fought at Waterloo . . .

Nor, on the other hand, are the passages here questioned, and others like them, instances of the lowered tension in writing such as we often find introduced with artistic propriety into narrative poetry. They are, rather, indications that the poet is momentarily relaxed in creative attention, and borrowing, and from a bad source at that. Other examples may be found, by those who care to look for them, in both *Locksley Halls*', and in a way, though less evidently and with more excuse, from such amusing exercises as the Northern Farmer poems.

Tis'n them as 'as munny as breäks into 'ouses an' steäls,
Them as 'as coäts to their backs an' taäkes their regular meäls.
Noä, but it's them as niver knaws wheer a meäl's to be 'ad.
Taäke my word for it, Sammy, the poor in a loomp is bad.

That has humorous charm, and as a *tour de force* in writing its merit is obvious. But it comes something short of poetry, because it is fundamentally an expression which is not natural to the poet. It is witty and extremely sensitive reporting, but it is no more, in so far, that is to say, as the diction is concerned, the selective and shaping power of art not being here in question. In saying that poetic language should be based on common idiom, we mean an idiom that is naturally within the poet's range, part of his own expressive habit, not an idiom that he deliberately copies. The Northern Farmer poems remain brilliant strokes of virtuosity, but Tennyson the poet had very little to do with them. It must be repeated, however, that in the great body of his work that explores the world of his own emotions, his response to nature and his simple but ever-brooding speculation, there is hardly a hint of the journalist confusing the poet.

Tennyson in relation to the fourth of our problems, that of allowing natural objects to call up ready-shaped images in association from the stores of poetry, has already been briefly considered in connection with his faded leaf and falling chestnut. And in this matter he was no more troubled when the content of his poetry was something other than natural description and its inferences. He writes—

> And I would that my tongue could utter
> The thoughts that arise in me . . .

but so intent is the mood that the siren voices of literature are beyond hearing, and on a sea unruffled by any alien wind

> the stately ships go on
> To their haven under the hill.

E

When Tennyson first published his poetry—
or the more significant part of his juvenile
poetry—there would be little to impress itself
as remarkable originality of style, and this was
as it should be. It is only the eccentric in art
that arrests garrulous attention, an attention
that has no memory. But the readers of the
volumes of 1830 and 1833 could not but be
aware that here was the old faculty speaking
with a note of new personality, an impression
to be strikingly confirmed in 1842. This was
English poetry plainly enough, quite content
to give tradition its due, properly proud of its
ancestry, and yet it was the work of a man
deeply engaged, indeed almost reclusively so,
in the artistic ordering of his own spiritual
life. In so far as he satisfactorily solved the
technical problems that have been mentioned,
he did so by a subconscious instinct of the
creative mind—they cannot, it is needless to
say, have appeared to him in the simple tabu-
lation that we are able to give them at this
distance of time. But the instinct that performed this office for him told him too that in
drawing freely upon the tradition of English
versification he must also add to it to be justified
of his calling. This is true of every poet, but
Tennyson knew it more decidedly, or at least
more explicitly, than most. Tennyson's subject
matter could not well have been more unsophisti-

cated, less affected by the challenge of the
spiritual experience of the great poets who
preceded him; but at the same time his style
could not well have been more manipulated,
more meticulously and self-consciously wrought
into the highest excellence that he could attain.
The picture of Tennyson as a " poet of the file,"
forever labouring in a lapidarian discontent,
is, perhaps, one that has been overdrawn, but
hardly any creative faculty of the first rank in
poetry has ever been so pervaded by the mood
of the artificer. Nothing could be wider of the
truth than to argue that the poise and balance
and perfect dovetailing that mark all his best
versification are merely so much decoration, a
kind of seductive jugglery that used up good
energy that might have been better employed.
It was his peculiar distinction as a poetic
craftsman that he was able to work his style
to the highest pitch of minutely considered
arrangement without sacrificing anything of
spontaneity in effect.

The stanzas quoted from *The Lady of Shalott*
show something of Tennyson's deftness in the
disposition of his words. A more matured
example is this from *The Princess*—

> Now sleeps the crimson petal, now the white;
> Nor waves the cypress in the palace walk;
> Nor winks the gold fin in the porphyry font :
> The firefly wakens ; waken thou with me.

Now droops the milk-white peacock like a ghost,
And like a ghost she glimmers on to me.

Now lies the Earth all Danaë to the stars,
And all thy heart lies open unto me.

Now slides the silent meteor on, and leaves
A shining furrow, as thy thoughts in me.

Now folds the lily all her sweetness up,
And slips into the bosom of the lake :
So fold thyself, my dearest, thou, and slip
Into my bosom and be lost in me :

A good deal has been said by critics about Tennyson's mastery over vowel and consonantal movement, but, in the light of such instances as this, certainly not more than enough, and in these later days at least rather less, I think, than is due. It is easy for unsympathetic criticism to see nothing but manufactured verse in this poem, but it is always easy for unsympathetic criticism to be stupidly unjust. This is not merely fine writing, it is style, and not to allow this is to be wanton about Tennyson altogether. Whatever personal taste may say, considered judgment should not permit itself to be blinded thus by partialities. That the artistry in these lines is deliberate, proving itself at every word, indeed at every letter, is unquestionable, but it is equally clear that the fusion of a poetic mood into this limpidly composed expression is complete. The perfect packing

or building of the words, as though they had
something of the quality of solid material in
them, was for Tennyson an actual means of
expression, and one in which he has never been
excelled, and, perhaps, never equalled. Under
analysis two lines in the poem call for separate
comment.

Nor winks the gold fin in the porphyry font

is exquisitely done, but detraction might protest
that it is just a shade too assertively picturesque,
and there is, moreover, for once a definite
reminiscence of Keats with his " beaded bubbles
winking at the brim." The line is, in some odd
way, almost too good. Then we have that
other one,

Now lies the Earth all Danaë to the stars,

which stands out by itself, as it would do in
any context, by sheer imaginative power. But
the poem for the rest is a normal illustration of
Tennyson's method. The verbal opulence is
peculiarly his own. It is not like that of Keats,
such as he uses in many passages of *The Eve of
St. Agnes*, where the inspiration is an almost
swooning delight in tropical colours and spiced
odours and textures very mellow to the touch.
Keats aimed at and succeeded marvellously in
finding in words some equivalence for these

sensations, but with Tennyson the artistic
intention was to arrest some almost impalpable
property in the words themselves. When we
charge a poet with merely using words we can
only mean that he is using impoverished words.
To complain that Tennyson overestimated the
power of words to give up some remote, and as
it were almost independent, life of their own to
the poet's incantation, is to complain that he
presumed to look upon language as in itself a
source of poetic life, which was no very wild
thing for a poet to do, since life, like God, does
move in a mysterious way. " Now droops the
milk-white peacock like a ghost," " Now slides
the silent meteor on," " Now folds the lily all
her sweetness up, And slips into the bosom of
the lake "—these words are revealing something at Tennyson's touch that they had kept
to themselves before. What precisely it is we
cannot say, because it exists only in terms of
Tennyson's divine manipulation. We can talk,
rationally enough, about vowels and consonants,
but we are still compelled to leave something
unsaid. But we miss much of the essential
Tennyson if we do not recognise that in his
orchestration of language he was, in a sense
almost peculiar to himself among poets,
creating life. " The chestnut pattering to the
ground," already quoted, may be given as

another case in point. "Pattering" is here something more than the best word in the usual sense. It is true that it is more precise than "falling," or "dropping," but when that margin of superiority is allowed for there is still something over. And that something is not a lucky but inessential grace; it is life, and life of Tennyson's especial engendering.

This, was, I think, Tennyson's particular enrichment of the tradition that he took up. A few other poets, Rossetti, for example, and others less celebrated, such as de Tabley, caught something of the way of it, but on the whole it was a very personal thing, perfected by its originator,* and not having any lasting influence. With Tennyson came and went the vital undertone of such lines as—

> The moan of doves in immemorial elms,
> The murmuring of innumerable bees.

If it was heard again it could be as an echo only.

* This is not to deny the quality to every poet before Tennyson, obviously. But never before had it been so salient a characteristic of a poetic style, nor has it been since.

V

O lyric love, half-angel and half-bird
And all a wonder and a wild desire,—
Boldest of hearts that ever braved the sun,
Took sanctuary within the holier blue,
And sang a kindred soul out to his face,—
Yet human at the red-ripe of the heart—
When the first summons from the darkling earth
Reach'd thee amid thy chambers, blanch'd their blue,
And bared them of the glory—to drop down,
To toil for man, to suffer or to die,—

Not considering the content matter, but looking alone at the way of writing, there is a clear
resemblance between this celebrated passage
from Browning and any characteristic example
of Tennyson's maturer manner. Tennyson
might have hesitated at " red-ripe of the heart,"
and have avoided the repetition of " blue " at
the end of a line, but otherwise there is nothing
either beyond or below his reach in Browning's
full-bodied and admirably balanced blank
verse. Nor was Browning incapable of the
richly-vestured lyric movement of which
Tennyson was a master—as this from *Paracelsus*
may show—

And strew faint sweetness from some old
    Egyptian's fine worm-eaten shroud
Which breaks to dust when once unroll'd;
    Or shredded perfume, like a cloud
From closet long to quiet vow'd,

> With moth'd and dropping arras hung,
> Mouldering her lute and books among,
> As when a queen, long dead, was young.

And then we pass from these, done so to speak by a master in the best manner of his age, to—

> I want to know a butcher paints,
> A baker rhymes for his pursuit,
> Candlestick-maker much acquaints
> His soul with song, or, haply mute,
> Blows out his brains upon the flute. . . .

and we seem almost to be listening to a different voice. Many poets have written in more than one manner. Tennyson himself had his familiar style, the poem written in his old age to FitzGerald, for example, which is as distinct from his graver manner as was the Keats of the Mermaid lines from the Keats of the Odes, or Milton in the verses to Hobson the carrier from himself in *Samson Agonistes*. But in these other cases the more colloquial manner is deliberately assumed for some occasion of lowered poetic pressure, not in the least unworthy or trivial, but of less imaginative urgency than " this great argument," while with Browning it becomes, no less than his greater ceremony, a serious poetic style, and one that as time went by more and more governed his practice. But Browning did not stay at the point indicated by " I want to know

a butcher paints." So far he was in some
measure, and more than any other major poet,
following the example of Byron, and replacing
poetic elevation—using the word in its original
sense—by a racy conversationalism. He was,
fairly enough, basing his poetic style upon common idiom, but the common idiom of his use
was rather evangelised into poetic efficiency
than distilled into poetic purity. Before he
could conceivably have written " blows out his
brains upon the flute " Tennyson would have
been seen consciously putting his singing robes
aside, but it came from Browning in full dress.
But the unequivocal use of witty tap-room
rhetoric, or call it what you will, was not all,
nor, be it said, was it in Browning's handling
an easy or undistinguished thing. This was in
no sense mere reporting. Before the idiom got
into his verse it was subjected to a very keen
intellectual scrutiny and ordering, but when it
did get there it was still far more recognisably
itself than was common in poetry. When,
however, we come upon such lines as—

> Hobbs hints blue,—straight he turtle eats :
> Nobbs prints blue,—claret crowns his cup :
> Nokes outdares Stokes in azure feats,—
> Both gorge. Who fished the murex up ?
> What porridge had John Keats ?

which we frequently do, though this famous

passage is admittedly an extreme case, we
have to deal with something more than the
direct removal of common idiom into verse.
Apart from actual obscurity of meaning, we
have here a poetic style that is strangely
elusive in its origin. It is useless to dismiss it
as being the mere vagary of a great but wilful
poet. Browning in this and many similar
passages was deliberately carrying out some
technical purpose, and, directed by some
instinct or another, was shaping his material
as he wished, and not being beaten by it.
At the beginning of this essay I suggested that
Browning's distinctive choice of diction was
controlled by a feeling, dominating him more
and more, that the poetical resources of the
language along traditional lines were for the
moment exhausted—clearly as he himself
disproved the belief in such work as " O lyric
love " and " And strew faint sweetness." For
the sake of convenience in this argument we
may speak—quite arbitrarily I admit—of
Browning's three characteristics as Tennysonian, Byronic, and the specifically Browningesque,* not chronologically but in character.
He was not exclusively engaged in any one of

* Let me repeat that this is for immediate purposes of definition only. Browning's individual mark
is clear enough upon his poetry right through.

these at a given time, but taking the body of
his mature work as a whole, it might be said
that its common measure is the second of these
manners, often brightened by an imaginative
strain from the first, and sometimes complicated by the third.   This range and variety in
his verse remained strictly within his style—
it was not a case of style too often subject to
manneristic contortions, as has sometimes been
suggested. Browning in his manner as well
as in his investigation was a very cosmopolitan
poet, and he could pass in a single poem from
one decided accent to another without any sense
of incongruity. This being so, it may be said
that the "Browningesque" quality in my
category is less typically Browning than the
others; the definition should, perhaps, be
qualified by adding that it is a quality that he
brings from a source of his own unaided discovery into the texture of a style emphatically
his own and yet inseparable from tradition.
Shop, from which the painting butcher and
rhyming baker come, shows the three strains
blended into a perfectly satisfactory whole.
This is the end of the poem.

> And whither went he?   Ask himself,
>   Not me! To change of scene, I think.
> Once sold the ware and pursed the pelf,
>   Chaffer was scarce his meat and drink,
>   Nor all his music—money-chink.

Because a man has shop to mind
    In time and peace, since flesh must live,
Needs spirit lack all life behind,
    All stray thoughts, fancies fugitive,
    All loves except what trade can give?

I want to know a butcher paints,
    A baker rhymes for his pursuit,
Candlestick-maker much acquaints
    His soul with song, or, haply mute,
    Blows out his brains upon the flute.

But—shop each day and all day long!
    Friend, your good angel slept, your star
Suffered eclipse, fate did you wrong!
    For where these sorts of treasures are
    There should our hearts be—Christ, how far!

Here we have the romantic richness, the direct
conversational idiom, and the crabbed Hobbs-
Nobbs figure all in one. And this last in Browning's work was, I think, a further development
of his dissatisfaction with the habit of verse as
he found it in general use. If the " elevated "
manner seemed to him to be exhausted, the
colloquial manner that he adopted as an alter-
native may very well soon have seemed to
him to be too flat and commonplace, to lack
the spring of good poetic writing, and it was a
natural thing for his genius to enliven it not by
a return to the accepted manner only—though
he did this as well—but also by inventing a
new complex of the common idiom, fantastic,

involved, and striking, if sometimes only by its oddity, yet always alert and personal. " I want to know a butcher paints " is the idiom of ordinary speech lifted bodily into poetry with the slightest of sea-changes; " O lyric love " is the same idiom ennobled and intensified, transfigured in the traditional way by a poetic master; in Nokes and Stokes and their azure feats is again the same idiom, but now vexed into an attitude, not in the least insincerely, but by a poet who has bravely but wilfully cut the old moorings and finds new ones very far to seek. Nothing could be less just than to accuse Browning of deliberate antics, but if, even for the most disinterested reasons, you forsake solid earth for the tight-rope you cannot help performing with the pole, and you are lucky if you get across even at that, which it must be allowed Browning generally did. I said that the stanzas from *Shop* showed the three strains in his style satisfactorily blended, but it would perhaps be nearer to the truth to say that they show them in close association, each contributing to a satisfactory whole, and kept by Browning's art from striking any discord, shown by him, in short, equally to be natural and congruous elements in the unity of his style. As showing these elements more indistinguishably combined

worked into one texture, three stanzas may
be given from *A Toccata of Galuppi's*—

Did young people take their pleasure when the sea
    was warm in May?
Balls and masks begun at midnight, burning ever
    to mid-day
When they made up fresh adventures for the morrow
    do you say?

Was a lady such a lady, cheeks so round and lips so
    red,—
On her neck the small face buoyant, like a bell-flower
    on its bed,
O'er the breasts superb abundance where a man
    might base his head?

Well (and it was graceful of them), they'd break talk
    off and afford
—She, to bite her mask's black velvet, he, to finger
    on his sword,
While you sat and play'd Toccatas, stately at the
    clavichord?

It will, perhaps, be found that this composite
style of Browning's invention is of all in the
Victorian age the one that has had most
influence upon the poetry of our own time.

VI

Broadly speaking, Tennyson and Browning
have come in general opinion to stand as the
two chief figures in Victorian poetry. Personal

revisions of this estimate are constantly being
made, and often with much critical weight.
But on the whole, and considering everything
that goes to the making of permanence in
poetic reputations, it is doubtful whether the
popular impression will not continue to hold
the day. In detail the debate is an endless
one, nor, so far as mere comparison is concerned, is it a very profitable one. I for one
find Matthew Arnold, for instance, a more
rewarding poet, with less waste tissue in his
work, and as time goes on richer in undis-
covered country than either Tennyson or
Browning, but I should not allow my personal
preference to place him above them in poetic
rank—the evidence against me is too weighty
for that. In the matter of diction which we
have been discussing, for example, in so far as
poets can affect their own age, Tennyson and
Browning were beyond question the two most
considerable influences of their time. Tennyson showed his generation, in a degree unap-
proached by any other poet who began writing
with him, the still fresh and vital possibilities
of a great traditional manner. Browning with
equal authority demonstrated what were the
likeliest methods of departure and revolt from
that manner. It is true that while Tennyson's
example modified the versification of many

poets in his own age, Browning's, though perhaps a more durable one, was far less immediate
in its effect. There was a definitely Tennysonian school, a number of accomplished and
genuine poets who would almost certainly have
written differently if it had not been for the
direct influence of the master, who, moreover,
considerably affected the poetic expression of
many, indeed of most, of his more celebrated
contemporaries. Here are a few instances from
the school—

(a) Come, let us mount the breezy down
    And hearken to the tumult blown
Up from the champaign and the town.*

(b) He roam'd half-round the world of woe,
    Where toil and labour never cease;
Then dropp'd one little span below
    In search of peace.

And now to him mild beams and showers,
    All that he needs to grace his tomb,
From loneliest regions at all hours,
    Unsought for, come.†

(c) As ships, becalm'd at eve, that lay
    With canvas drooping, side by side,
Two towers of sail at dawn of day
    Are scarce, long leagues apart, descried;

* Frederick Tennyson.
† Aubrey de Vere (the younger).

F

When fell the night, upsprung the breeze,
    And all the darkling hours they plied,
Nor dreamt but each the self-same seas
    By each was cleaving, side by side :

E'en so—but why the tale reveal
    Of those, whom year by year unchanged,
Brief absence join'd anew to feel,
    Astounded, soul from soul estranged ? *

(*d*) They told me, Heraclitus, they told me you were
    dead,
They brought me bitter news to hear and bitter
    tears to shed.
I wept as I remember'd how often you and I
Had tired the sun with talking and sent him
    down the sky.

And now that thou art lying, my dear old Carian
    guest,
A handful of grey ashes, long, long ago at rest,
Still are thy pleasant voices, thy nightingales,
    awake;
For Death, he taketh all away, but them he cannot
    take.†

---

  * Arthur Hugh Clough. Tennyson would have avoided the repeated rhyme sounds of the first and second stanzas, and the third, given here for the sense, is below standard.

  † *Heraclitus*, by William Cory. Cory (Johnson by birth) was a very occasional poet, but when he wrote like this Tennyson himself could have done it no better, although no less an authority than Professor Gilbert Murray, in an instructive paper on verse translation, has recently complained, quite unaccountably as it seems to me, that the poem fails by reason of triviality in diction and rhythm.

(*e*) The feathers of the willow
    Are half of them grown yellow
      Above the swelling stream;
And ragged are the bushes,
And rusty now the rushes,
      And wild the clouded gleam.

The thistle now is older,
His stalks begin to moulder,
      His head is white as snow;
The branches all are barer,
The linnet's song is rarer.
      The robin pipeth low.*

(*f*) O tender dove, sweet circling in the blue,
Whom now a delicate cloud receives from view,
A cool, soft, delicate cloud, we name dim Death !
O pure white land-lily, inhaling breath
From spiritual ether among bowers
Of evergreen in the ever-living flowers
Yonder aloft upon the airy height,
Mine eyes may scarce arrive at thy still light ! †

(*g*) Hear, O ye Lemnians, hear a full brief word
Before I go, for surely from this day
My voice shall be a silence on your rocks,
My face a dimness with a few old men
Remembered hardly. As day fathers day
'Tis meet my memory pass; ay, meet that all
Change and be changed. So roll the stars along
And the great world is crown'd with silent lights
Watching her changes, and no thing endures.‡

---

* Richard Watson Dixon.
† Roden Noel.
‡ Lord de Tabley.

I need hardly say that I do not suggest that
the poets from whom these examples—almost
at random—are given, and many who could be
placed in their company, are merely imitators
of Tennyson. Men like Clough, Dixon, and
de Tabley were fine spirits finely touched to
song. Clough, to speculate idly, with a little
more energy, might have found his way into
the great group of his age. Dixon was a lyric
poet who has been eulogised by so fastidious a
critic as Mr. Bridges, which is warrant enough
for any man. And de Tabley constantly got
to the summits, only to find them too slippery
for long foothold. But, individual as these
and the others were in their gifts, the extracts
given are enough to show clearly how susceptible the poetry of the age was to Tennyson's
diction. Generally speaking, this was all to
the good. Predominating influences are inevitable among any generation of poets, and it
was no bad fortune for a large number of the
Victorians to find so good a preceptor. With
one possible exception, everything that these
poets of real but not commanding achievement
got from Tennyson was gain. They took from
him no eccentricity, but each according to his
own powers something of his new interpretation of a tradition that was the common heri-
tage. The possible exception was de Tabley,

who, the more he is read, the more he impresses
with his very rare potentialities. He, perhaps,
alone among the poets of anything like his
natural endowment, made at times too complete a surrender to example. A careful study
of his verse convinces me that the lapses from
excellence, of which it is in danger at every
turn, are almost entirely the result of an
habitual recollection, in relaxed moods, of
Tennyson's manner, which in happier moments
influenced him wholly for good. If, as I have
already suggested, he more than the others
could sometimes catch the particular enchantment in Tennyson's use of words, the enchantment that save for a stray note here and there
came and went with the master, he also suffered
more than the others by reason of his very
sensibility. He could write—

> Say what you will and have your sneer and go.
> You see the specks, we only need the fruit
> Of a great life, whose truth—men hate truth so—
> No lukewarm age of compromise could suit.
> Laugh and be mute !

but he could also write—

> "And what is Love by nature?"
> My pretty true-love sighs.
> And I reply, in feature
> A child with pensive eyes.

> An infant forehead shaded
> With many ringlet rings,
> And pearly shoulders faded
> In the colour of his wings.

Before returning to Browning, we may consider the influence that Tennyson further had —Tennyson, that is again to say, as representing the age's normal modification of tradition— upon the diction of the more celebrated poets of the Victorian era. Matthew Arnold published his first book—*The Strayed Reveller and other Poems* (apart from prize poems at Rugby and Oxford) in 1849, when he was twenty-seven years of age, and his second, *Empedocles on Etna*, three years later. So little attention was paid to books that contained some of the loveliest poetry of a century, that their author successively withdrew each of them from publication when a few copies had gone out, and they have become bibliographical treasures. With the two volumes of *Poems*, 1853 and 1855, however, he took his place among the acknowledged poets of the time, and although he has never been everybody's poet, he has never since then been without admirers who would hardly admit any of his contemporaries as his better. The nature of his poetry will be referred to in the proper place, but its diction is of great importance in a study of the age's versifica-

tion. Professor Saintsbury * (who is just a
little inclined to stand for the illiberal estimate
of Arnold as a poet) says " he is most con-
sistent in employing, or at least endeavouring
to employ, a severer kind of diction and versification, drawing itself back from the florid
and flowing Tennysonian scheme towards the
stiffer movement and graver tones of Wordsworth, Gray, and (in his later years) Milton."
This is very perspicuous, but the very fact that
there was in Arnold's style something of a
conscious drawing back from Tennyson's
manner implies that the influence of the older
poet was by no means without its effect, and
we shall find plainly that this was so.   The fact
is that Tennyson, " florid and flowing " as he
may have been at times, was far from unconscious in much of his finest work of those
models to whom Arnold is said to have turned
by way of escape as it were.   Neither Milton
nor Gray nor Wordsworth could have written
more gravely-toned than this, the Tennyson of
Ulysses—

* I have not in general much use for criticism
that quotes other criticism, but at this time of day
anyone may steal from the stores of Professor Saintsbury's learning and wisdom, and although there is no
modern critic, perhaps, so provocative as he, there is
none who has left his mark so indelibly upon every
subsequent judgment of English poetry.

It may be that the gulfs will wash us down :
It may be we shall touch the Happy Isles,
And see the great Achilles, whom we knew.
Tho' much is taken, much abides ; and tho'
We are not now the strength which in old days
Moved earth and heaven ; that which we are, we are ;
One equal temper of heroic hearts,
Made weak by time and fate, but strong in will
To strive, to seek, to find, and not to yield. . . .

and, on the other hand, it is impossible to
miss Tennyson's modification of those models
in much of Arnold's representative poetry, or
at least not to be aware that Arnold's own
instinct is moving in the same direction.

Alack, for Corydon no rival now !—
But when Sicilian shepherds lost a mate,
    Some good survivor with his flute would go,
Piping a ditty sad for Bion's fate,
    And cross the unpermitted ferry's flow,
        And relax Pluto's brow,
And make leap up with joy the beauteous head
    Of Proserpine, among whose crownèd hair
    Are flowers, first open'd on Sicilian air,
And flute his friend, like Orpheus, from the dead.

If that is a return to an older manner, it is an
older manner with a difference, and the difference is one that in the first place was of Tennyson's invention. Arnold was too personal a
poet not to invest even his acquired characteristics with his own stamp, but when we read

verse like this we know that Milton, Gray and
Wordsworth were not the only masters. And,
in fact, Tennyson's particular " linked sweetness long drawn out " was not more certainly
achieved by its originator himself than by
Arnold in such passages as—

> Too quick despairer, wherefore wilt thou go?
> Soon will the high Midsummer pomps come on,
> Soon will the musk carnations break and swell,
> Soon shall we have gold-dusted snapdragon. . . .

and

> Thee, at the ferry, Oxford riders blithe,
>   Returning home on summer nights, have met
> Crossing the stripling Thames at Bablock-hithe,
>   Trailing in the cool stream thy fingers wet. . . .

and

> Its melancholy, long, withdrawing roar,
> Retreating to the breath
> Of the night-wind down the vast edges drear
> And naked shingles of the world. . . .

and

>   Dost thou once more assay
> Thy flight, and feel come over thee,
> Poor Fugitive, the feathery change
> Once more, and once more seem to make resound
> With love and hate, triumph and agony,
> Lone Daulis, and the high Cephissian vale?
>   Listen, Eugenia—

How thick the bursts come crowding through the
    leaves !
  Again—thou hearest !
  Eternal Passion !
  Eternal Pain !

Instances could be multiplied : they abound
in Arnold's poetry. It is true that Arnold did,
more perhaps than any other poet of his time,
bring back into verse something of the hard,
jade-like, quality in a phrase that was characteristic of Milton, and almost even more so
of Donne, Vaughan and many seventeenth-
century lyrists, in a smaller degree of Gray and
Wordsworth, hardly attempted by Keats, and
less by Tennyson. It was a quality, it may
perhaps be said, borrowed by poetry from the
great prose writers such as Jeremy Taylor and
Thomas Browne and Izaak Walton. It is a
subtle quality, one difficult to get at or define,
a very attractive thing when well used, and
yet a quality to which many good poets are
indifferent. When Tennyson writes, " His
captain's ear has heard them boom Bellowing
victory, bellowing doom," and Browning " And
yonder soft phial, the exquisite blue," and
Aubrey de Vere " while such perfect sound
Fell from his bowstring," and Poe " Lo, in
yon brilliant window-niche," and Longfellow
" We can make our lives sublime," and Brown-

ing again " There's heaven above, and night by
night, I look right through its gorgeous roof,"
the words bellowing, exquisite, perfect, brilliant (though Poe very nearly justifies himself),
sublime, and gorgeous are all words badly
used in poetry, mere counters taken lazily from
the fingered stock of prose.* It is precisely
the poet's business to translate such words as
these into poetry, to recreate the things that
they stand for in the looseness of common
talk, and not to take them over with all their
imperfections on them. In conversation, even
in written prose, they have their place and are
well enough, but in poetry they won't do—
though most poets have blundered in this matter
at one time or another. It is not a case of
forbidding the poet simple and commonplace
words; these he may use as often as he will,
if he can use them with mastery. He may say
the moon is bright, because that means something definite, but he may not say the moon
is exquisite, because that does not mean anything definite at all. And he may not even
say the moon is brilliant—or at least not with
any safety — because brilliant only means
bright, which is definite, plus a qualification

* Each reader may have his quarrel with my instances. But they served an argument that seemed
worth pursuing.

which is quite indefinite; it pretends to say something more than bright, but leaves us uninformed as to what the something more is, and so becomes a pretentious word. If the poet wants to emphasise the brightness he can do so by means of an image, or even by saying very bright, if he can, as sometimes he can, beguile us into honouring the " very " by rhythmic cunning. But " brilliant " in poetry is inorganic. Sublime, bellowing, gorgeous and the rest of them belong to a large group of words that are over-specific or under-specific in meaning for poetry. " Bellowing " implies a very particular kind of loud noise, but that particularity is of no significance, and all that the word gives us in Tennyson's verse over and above, say, " sounding," is something that it is not worth while to give; it is too specific, so that in poetry it acquires a certain kind of fatuity. " Gorgeous," on the other hand, is not specific enough. The margin of meaning in it beyond some such word as bright or starry or shining or, perhaps, encrusted, is something known only vaguely to each person as he uses it, and not communicated in any definite way by the word itself. " Gorgeous roof " means nothing, in the sense that it is poetry's obliga-tion to mean something, that is not accounted for by " starry roof." The added meaning

remains something secret to Browning. It is of
no use in this connection to talk about poetry
being " suggestive." The suggestive power of
poetry should be something that compels us to
an effort of the mind that results in the creation
of a clear-cut image, not something directing us
into a world of vague sensations and guesswork.

Before proceeding to the next step in the
analysis of the quality that I have claimed for
Arnold, there is another group of words to
be considered that might at first thought seem
to be of the same kind as those just mentioned.
Perhaps " magnificent " is as good an example
as any. Why, it may be asked, should " magnificent " be suitable for poetic use if " gorgeous" is not? Clearly we are on very hazardous
ground, but the way is, I think, none the less
certain. We know that instinct has told the
common practice of poetry to accept the one
and to reject the other, and the instinct must
have had some source in reason. Admitting
that what we need in poetry is exact definition,
it can, I think, be shown that there is this
difference between the two words. " Gorgeous,"
in itself, means (let us say) " splendid " plus
some unknown degree of " splendour." It is
not a case of splendour of one kind plus—even
though it be in an unknown degree—splendour
of another. So that it depends for its very

particularity upon a meaning that finally escapes us, and not even Milton with his "Gorgeous Tragedy" can quite subdue it to his art. But with "magnificent" this is not so. The meaning is still "splendid" (let us say) plus something, but the something is not now merely an undefined further quantity of "splendour." It is, rather, a particular qualification of splendour which is derived from the context, and which, from that context, will nearly always be found to be imaginatively specific. Thus, when Wordsworth says—

Once did she hold the gorgeous East in fee . . .

the figure of " the East " is hardly emphasised at all by " gorgeous." " Splendid " alone would have done the work as well, and not have disturbed our sense of fitness by any pretentiousness. If Wordsworth, we feel, wanted to say more than that the East was splendid, to convey the distinguishing quality of that splendour, it was his business to do it somehow precisely, and not to evade his responsibility by using a word that, so far as qualification of " splendid " goes, leaves us in the air. And, from some subtle essence in its nature, the word " magnificent " would have served his turn. Had he said " the magnificent East," we should—or so it seems decisively to my perception—have received the idea of

" splendid " from the primary meaning of the
epithet, which epithet would in turn have, by
its peculiar evocative power, gathered to itself
from the context the explicit kind of splendour
of light and colour and jewelled opulence that
we associate with the East. The word " magnificent," in short, is an organic one in poetry,
while " gorgeous " is not. When Browning
speaks of " that pulse's magnificent come-
and-go," we get the image of glowing health
reinforced by the idea of a superb physical
power and functioning, conveyed through the
word " magnificent " in relation to " pulse."
" Splendid " here would have been measurably
less significant, while " gorgeous "—if we may
strain the word's meaning for the purpose of
illustration—would, in qualifying " splendid,"
have weakened the impression instead of
strengthening it. Again, as a last example,
Sir William Watson in his *Autumn* has, within
a few lines of each other—

> At thy mute signal, leaf by golden leaf,
> Crumbles the gorgeous year. . . .

and

> And passage and departure all thy theme,
> Whose life doth still a splendid dying seem,
> And thou, at height of thy magnificence,
> A figment and a dream. . . .

the one of which is nebulous and the other
shaped. And the language has many pairs

or groups of words, not necessarily synonymous but of a like character, that fall respectively into the " gorgeous " or " magnificent " class, as, for instance, valorous, heroic, and transparent, crystalline, and regrettable or deplorable as against lamentable or grievous, and vicious, malignant, and vague, dim, and conceited, vain, and expensive, costly, and so on. It is hardly safe to say of any word that it can never be used seriously in poetry, but of those given as belonging to the " gorgeous " group—there are hundreds like them—it can at least be said that poetry would almost always lose more than she would gain by them.

Arnold's gift of bringing a certain spare prose quality with profit into his poetry is not, therefore, to be observed in his use of such words as " magnificent " and the rest, which are naturally enough poetic, and not dangerous so long as they are kept clearly distinguished from the specifically prose " gorgeous " group. Nor, again, as we have seen, is it to be found in his control of such simplicities as " the sun is bright," since these also are—or can be in right usage—essentially poetic. Also it is a distinct thing from that other simplicity that relies at moments of almost overwhelming emotion upon an expression stripped of every syllable that can go and yet, throbbing with

momentum, having nothing in it of under-
statement; the kind of expression of which
Shakespeare was the supreme master—

> Soft you. A word or two before you go.
> I have done the state some service, and they know't.
> No more of that. . . .

and

> O ! that a man might know
> The end of this day's business, ere it come;
> But it sufficeth that the day will end
> And then the end is known . . .

and

> She should have died hereafter;
> There would have been a time for such a word. . . .

The quality of which we are speaking in Arnold
was, rather, a certain sudden tempering of the
diction in poetry, with magical result. It was
a quality that he more than any other poet
of his time recovered from the seventeenth
century, the age of poets like Vaughan and
Marvell who could lift us to the height of
poetic enjoyment with such prose-habited
devices as—

> Where no rude foot e'er trod,
> Where, since he walk'd there, only go
> Prophets and friends of God. . . .

and

> The grave's a fine and private place.

G

These are not at all in the same kind as " She should have died hereafter." They depend for their effect not upon the sudden release of vast cumulative passion, but upon the lovely—almost arrogant—draft upon commonplace, the perfectly judged use of " friends " and " fine " at their utterly unexpected but divinely appointed moments. And this effect Arnold could often come by, and the rest of the Victorians hardly ever. Here are two examples—

> I have a fretted brick-work tomb
> Upon a hill on the right hand,
> Hard by a close of apricots
> Upon the road to Samarcand.
>
> Thither, O Vizier, will I bear
> This man my pity could not save :
> And, plucking up the marble flags,
> There lay his body in my grave.
>
> Bring water, nard, and linen rolls,
> Wash off all blood, set smooth each limb.
> They say : " He was not wholly vile,
> Because a king shall bury him." . . .

and

> . . . and in his ears
> The murmur of a thousand years :
> Before him he sees Life unroll,
> A placid and continuous whole;
> That general Life, which does not cease,
> Whose secret is not joy, but peace;
> That Life, whose dumb wish is not miss'd
> If birth proceeds, if things subsist :

The Life of plants, and stones, and rain :
The Life he craves; if not in vain
Fate gave, what chance shall not control,
His sad lucidity of soul.

The instinct that led Arnold to such expression
as this was akin to an austerity, sometimes
stupidly confused with coldness, that is among
the rarest and most secluded of poetry's enchant-
ments, the austerity of which the poet himself
wrote—

Such, poets, is your bride, the Muse ! young, gay,
Radiant, adorn'd outside; a hidden ground
Of thought and of austerity within.

If Arnold stood in his age for a chastening
of the " florid and flowing " Tennysonian
manner, though less unequivocally so, perhaps,
than Professor Saintsbury would seem to
suggest, Dante Gabriel Rossetti, William Morris
and Swinburne, in their respective ways, carried
that manner to its extreme emphasis. This, I
need hardly say, does not mean that the style
of any of these men was exclusively derived
from Tennyson, but rather that the characteristic evolved by Tennyson from poetic tradition that warrants Professor Saintsbury's
" florid and flowing," was developed by these
younger poets into a poetic diction that was
drawn partly from Tennyson's own sources
and partly from Tennyson himself. Just as

the influence of Milton, Gray and Wordsworth upon Arnold was modified by the intervening practice of Tennyson, so was the influence of Chaucer, Spenser, Shelley, Byron and Keats in some measure affected by Tennyson before they reached Rossetti, Morris and Swinburne.

To set Rossetti's *Blessed Damozel* beside one of Tennyson's most highly decorative poems, *The Lady of Shalott,* for example, is to be aware of a new weight in an atmosphere already heavily charged. The graphic presentation of Tennyson's poem is wrought with great ingenuity of artifice, but the landscape, although it no longer has the rain-washed clarity of Chaucer, is still in the open air. The golden sheaves and the Camelot road and the lilied island have something of the brightness of unfaded tapestry, but they have something also of summer in Cornwall. In *The Blessed Damozel* we have passed out of day and night and are moving in a landscape of gold and blue and rose thickly laid on gesso and stuck over with precious stones. It glows through a mist of colour that is almost sensible to the touch, and has been passionately created, not by God in Cornwall, but by monks in mediæval cloisters. In Tennyson's poem there is the artifice of a very expert poetic craftsman, applied to a vision that is direct and material, in Rossetti's there is a genuine artificiality of imagination, expressing itself in a diction suffused with suggestion that is at once ethereal and strictly formal.

> The blessèd damozel lean'd out
>   From the gold bar of Heaven;
> Her eyes were deeper than the depth
>   Of waters still'd at even;
> She had three lilies in her hand,
>   And the stars in her hair were seven.

These are no waters of earth, nor are the lilies and the stars—the three and the seven—those of our familiar vision. The water is some pool beyond the well at the world's end, and the lilies and the stars are such as might have been held one in each hand by the Prologue to a fourteenth-century mystery play at the church porch.

> Herself shall bring us, hand in hand,
>   To Him round whom all souls
> Kneel, the clear-ranged unnumbered heads
>   Bowed with their aureoles :
> And angels meeting us shall sing
>   To their citherns and citoles.

It is not a sufficient explanation of this to say merely that Rossetti was a painter as well as a poet. Nor was it wholly that he, beyond the example of any poet before him, sought to wring the last voluptuous essence out of the very nature of words themselves. Nor, finally, was diction of this kind simply the inevitable consequence of the deliberate Pre-Raphaelite pact. Beyond all these contributory causes, there was in Rossetti a native distrust of common life, kept by his artistic vitality just this side of morbidity, that led him to the creation of a world, lustrous, brooding, its *fauna* and *flora* always a little fabulous, a world of murmured incantations and living heraldry. Here Rossetti suffered the pangs and gathered the compensations common to humanity, but his emotion, simple in character though it was, found its natural element in this embroidered and incense-laden world, and could not easily fulfil itself elsewhere. And in the diction of his poetry Rossetti delineated his world exactly, with its " twilit hidden glimmering visages." Hardly any other poet, I suppose, could have praised the beloved for her " sultry hair."

Morris was profoundly influenced by Rossetti in his art, and there was a close personal sympathy between them, and yet two poets could not well be more unlike each other in natural temperament. Rossetti's heavy-lidded indolence, his exotic preference for odd beasts in the garden, his savour of the apothecary's shop, were far removed from the robust world-

liness of Morris, who loved Socialist meetings,
and Cotswold winds, and the dye-vats in a
Staffordshire mill, and fishing for pike in the
Thames, and even a row in a police-court.
But the instinct for definite outline and exact
detail that made him whole-hearted in his
sympathy with the Pre-Raphaelite painters in
their revolt from what they considered to be a
smudgy and lazy impressionism, made him
also very susceptible to the luminous and
graphic quality of Rossetti's diction, and, in
that measure, guided him to his own development of the "florid and flowing" Tennysonian idiom. But once the impulse was working,
it sent Morris along his own way of discovery,
one upon which he had no company of importance. As he progressed in his art from *The
Lady of Shalott* and *The Blessed Damozel*, from
the lovely exercise of—

> Green holly in Alicia's hand,
> *When the Sword went out to sea,*
> With sere oak-leaves did Ursula stand;
> O! yet alas for me!
> I did but bear a peel'd white wand,
> *When the Sword went out to sea. . . .*

the world of mediæval and classic story became
less and less mere material for his poetry and
more and more the actual place of his habita-
tion. No poet has ever so utterly projected

himself into another age as did Morris. Much
has been written to show that Morris of *The
Earthly Paradise* and Morris of the political
platform were one and the same person, and
the doctrine cannot be lightly dismissed. But
in a sense Sigurd and Jason and Gudrun and
Atalanta were more vividly and intimately his
fellows than the chairman and committee and
the men and women of his audience. Though
he did not tell them so exactly in so many
words, his real ambition in going on to the
political platform at all was to persuade these
men and women that the Sigurds and the
Atalantas were really the best company in all
the world, and there willingly for their delight
if they would but know them. And in moving
among these people of a golden age (these
people, that is to say, as recorded by the
old poets, Chaucer and the *troubadours* and
trouvères) Morris not only steeped himself in
their physical and spiritual life, he very largely
caught and re-created the very manner of their
expression. He did something in the diction of
his poetry that had never before and is never
likely again to be attempted successfully, he
made an archaic idiom a living, personal, and
original thing. The complaint about " War-
dour Street " diction that has sometimes been
made against Morris is stupid and indefensible.

His poetic style may not please us in all moods,
but when we are prepared for it we see that,
unlikely as was his method to bring about such
an event by the light of experience, it is as
purely and individually a style as any poet's,
and that he has borrowed nothing without
transmuting it to the strict degree of his obliga-
tion.   When he follows Chaucer's example and
speaks of the brown bird, or the grey sky, or
the bright flowers, and leaves it at that, we
find ourselves accepting the image as complete,
so naturally does he adopt the accent of a
fourteenth-century poet and so far do we seem
from the nineteenth century merely imitating
the fourteenth.   And the whole of his diction
is radically modified by this circumstance,
thus—

Ah ! let me turn the page, nor chronicle
In many words the death of faith, or tell
Of meetings by the newly-risen moon,
Of passionate silence, 'midst the brown birds' tune,
Of wild tears wept within the noontide shade,
Of wild vows spoken that of old were made
For other ears, when, amidst other flowers,
He wandered through the love-begetting hours. . . .

and
                    At last
        Into an open space she passed,
        Nigh filled with a wide, shallow lake;
        Amidmost which the fowl did take
        Their pastime.

And even when his immediate concern, as in *The Message of the March Wind*, is with the life of an age that is his own by accident as it were, the manner still prevails—

Now sweet, sweet it is thro' the land to be straying,
'Mid the birds and the blossoms and the beasts of the
   field;
Love mingles with love, and no evil is weighing
On thy heart or mine, where all sorrow is heal'd.

From township to township, o'er down and by tillage
Far, far have we wander'd and long was the day;
But now cometh eve at the end of the village,
Where over the grey wall the church riseth grey.

Criticism may tell us that " the land " is an inadequate generalisation, that to say merely that it is " sweet " to be straying through it is to say nothing, that " the birds and the blossoms and the beasts " are poetic counters, that " where all sorrow is heal'd " is a sentimental *cliché* dragged in for purposes of rhyme, that " from township to township " makes no figure on the map, that " long was the day " is trite, and so on to its silly heart's content. But if, when it has finished, it fails to perceive the living spirit of poetry in those stanzas of Morris's, then we at least are not called upon to waste our energy in disputing the matter.

Tennyson's first book (excluding the *Poems*

by Two Brothers) was published in 1830,
Arnold's in 1849, Rossetti's in 1870, Morris's
in 1858, and Swinburne's in 1860, although
Atalanta in Calydon and *Poems and Ballads*,
by which volumes the character of his genius
first fully asserted itself, did not appear until
1865 and 1866 respectively. Rossetti was six
years older than Morris and eight years older
than Swinburne, but he kept his poems,
though they were well known to his friends,
unpublished in book-form for many years.
Among them all, Swinburne, the youngest, is
the most perplexing as a poet. Leaving the
content matter of his poetry for mention in
the proper place, we find in his manner the
apotheosis of the technique of an age, we might
almost say of many ages. With a poetic
scholarship as liberal as and more widely read
than Arnold's, an ear as sensitive to the
harmonics of words as Tennyson's, a gift of
incantation as befumed as Rossetti's, a sense
of romantic story as poignant and of English
landscape as tender and sparkling as was
Morris's, and a metrical virtuosity that was
unknown to any of them, or, indeed, to any
other English poet, Swinburne was, technically, at once the most unoriginal and the most
accomplished of the great men of his age. Of
the particular poetic beauty that we have

examined in Arnold—the beauty of " prophets
and friends of God "—he had nothing ; the spare
enchantment of the seventeenth-century lyric
was the one eminent grace in the stores of
English poetry that he did not gather up to his
own uses. He, again, went to the sources
partly through Tennyson, and, remembering
this, it would perhaps put the matter in a word
to say that it would be a safe undertaking to
match any particular excellence in Tennyson's
diction, or in that of any of the poets who
were influenced in Tennyson's direction, with
a corresponding excellence somewhere to be
found in the work of Swinburne.

Sleep; and if life were bitter to thee, pardon,
  If sweet, give thanks; thou hast no more to live;
  And to give thanks is good, and to forgive.
Out of the mystic and the mournful garden
  Where all day through thine hands in barren braid
  Wove the sick flowers of secrecy and shade,
Green buds of sorrow and sin, and remnants grey,
  Sweet smelling, pale with poison, sanguine-hearted,
  Passions that sprang from sleep and thoughts that
      started,
Shall death not bring us all as thee one day
  Among the days departed.

In a passage such as this, not considering
the nature of the content matter, and setting
aside qualities in the style peculiar to Swinburne, there is clearly sounded in the actual

writing the note that distinguished Victorian poetry from the poetry of earlier ages. The quality in this which is distinctively Swinburne's own, as it is in the great body of his work, is one in which the effect of metrical movement, or more precisely the play of metrical movement upon diction, is more important than it commonly was in the verse of his contemporaries. As I have suggested earlier in this essay, the technical originality of poetry by the time that Tennyson began to write, if not, indeed, before that, was to be sought rather in diction, the elements of which we have discussed, and in rhythmic currents moving along more or less established metrical channels, than in actual metrical invention. But Swinburne more than any other poet of his time calls for modification of this statement. To distinguish rhythmic beat from metrical pattern is difficult, perhaps impossible to do by any rule of thumb. But a careful examination of Swinburne's verse as a whole reveals that, in comparison with poets of his own stature, he had little rhythmic subtlety, a diction that was superbly copious but seldom touched with the rarer magic of discovery, and a metrical genius that, in its power, its variety and its essential artistic significance, may be said without over-statement to remain beyond the approach of any other English poet. While most people would, I think, accept the generalisation without question, in so far as it concerns Swinburne's diction, they might question it in respect of rhythm and metre. The average reader of poetry, whose business rightly is to enjoy what he is reading before coming to a close analysis of its nature, should he come to that at all, if asked what most struck him in Swinburne's poetry would probably say that it was its rich and intoxicating rhythm. The trained critical mind, on the other hand, might assert that, masterly as Swinburne's metrical performance was, it was hardly ever metrical invention. Both would be difficult to answer, and yet I think both might be persuaded. We have only to take any characteristic passage from one of the supreme creators of rhythmical life, such as Shakespeare and Milton and Wordsworth and Keats and Tennyson and Arnold, and to see how nervously the phrasing line runs through it, to realise how little of this line there is in Swinburne, and that the beat which rings so seductively or impressively in our ears from *The Garden of Proserpine* and *The Forsaken Garden* and the *Atalanta* choruses and a hundred other splendid poems, is really a metrical beat and not a rhythmical beat at all. And on the other hand, while it would be dangerous to say that any single metrical form used by Swinburne could not be shown to have its model in an older use, his metrical abundance and ingenuity are so great, the new combinations he makes so many and fortunate, the effect he produces so incisive and unforgettable, that his use of metre may reasonably enough be allowed as an original achievement of genius. It is not difficult to support the whole position by a single poem or, indeed, by two stanzas of a single poem.

Let us go hence, my songs; she will not hear.
Let us go hence together without fear;
Keep silence now, for singing-time is over,
And over all old things and all things dear.
She loves not you nor me as all we love her.
Yea, though we sang as angels in her ear,
    She would not hear.

Let us rise up and part; she will not know
Let us go seaward as the great winds go,
Full of blown sand and foam; what help is here?
There is no help, for all these things are so,
And all the world is bitter as a tear.
And how these things are, though ye strive to show,
    She would not know. . . .

That is technically a sheer triumph of metrical skill. Of the rhythmic line of which we have spoken there is nothing. Of the finer enchantment of diction also there is nothing. In fourteen lines there are over a hundred mono-

syllabic words, and it could hardly be claimed
for one of them that they perform any magical
evocation, such as do those words quoted of
Vaughan and Marvell. The monosyllabic commonplace of the diction is hardly redeemed by
the few words that have some stock poetic association, and the diction is, indeed, in itself as insignificant as the rhythm. And yet this is lovely
verse, among the best work of a great poet,
and its virtue comes from its exquisite metrical
authority. So pronounced is this that the
absence of rhythmical vitality does not matter,
being made good by a metrical beauty that
under this poet's direction is in itself something
as satisfying. And the poverty of the diction
is no longer poverty, taking from the metrical
genius of the verse all that it needs of colour
and temperament. Swinburne's characteristic
contribution to the poetic technique of his age
was to show that great verse could be produced
without the greatest gifts of rhythm or diction. He had an ear that was, in one sense,
faultless, but it rarely caught the long haunting
undertones of poetry that flow about the
structure of most great verse, and he could
command every device of verbal luxuriance
without being able to penetrate to the last
spiritual recesses of language. What, with all
his powers, he lacked of greatness in these

respects, he made good by his one unchallenged mastery. Since of the three elements of poetic technique, metre, rhythm and diction, metre is least inscrutable in its nature, it followed that Swinburne was at once fatally easy of imitation and less influential than any of his peers upon the living tradition of English poetry. Dozens of poets have written very like Swinburne, but no poet has ever written better because of him.

VII

So much for the Tennysonian influence upon Victorian technique, and the questions arising from the work of poets who were subject to, or part of, that influence. The manner which we have examined as being characteristically Browning's made a far less marked impression upon the work of his age. It can hardly be said of any of the greater poets of the time that he wrote differently because of Browning's example. There are notes in some of Morris's early work in which we can detect a moment's consciousness of the Browning idiom—in *Sir Peter Harpdon's End* for instance—but it passed never to return, and is nowhere else to be found in the principal poets of the time, with one exception to be mentioned. Browning's influence upon later poetry is another matter, but not one for discussion here, where it must

H

be sufficient to repeat that in the new vigour that came into English poetry after the perfumed dusk of the eighteen-nineties * Browning is likely to be found by critical historians to have had a considerable hand. Of the less celebrated Victorian poets, who were yet in some measure an adornment of their age, three found in Browning's technique a more constant inspiration to their own. These were Richard Hengist Horne, Alfred Domett and T. E. Brown. Horne was a strange figure in Victorian poetry who gets an obscure corner in the anthologies, and is otherwise forgotten save as a friend of the Brownings. But he was a poet of great ambitions, and of a good deal more achievement than we remember. His epic poem *Orion*, which attained much fame in its time, and some permanent notoriety as the Farthing Epic, so called because Horne, angered by public neglect when it first appeared, contemptuously had it sold at a farthing, is a very readable work for anyone who cares to try it and is not afraid of poetry in long measure. Also he wrote many admirable short pieces, and his work as a whole only needed more of

* This, I need not say, is a very partial definition of a decade that was not exclusively represented by the sallow genius of an Ernest Dowson and an Aubrey Beardsley.

the discipline that would have kept him from
sprawling in poetry to have given him a much
wider reputation than he now enjoys. He was
an older man than Browning, having been born
in 1803, but he lived a long working life of
eighty years, and so far as he made his poetic
mark in either direction it was rather in
Browning's than in Tennyson's. *The Plough*,
justly the best known of his lyrics, has a kind
of ungarlanded earthiness and an impetus in
its conclusion that remind us rather of Browning's robust method than of the more opulent
tendencies of the age.

Above yon sombre swell of land
    Thou see'st the dawn's grave orange hue,
With one pale streak like yellow sand,
    And over that a vein of blue.

The air is cold above the woods;
    All silent is the earth and sky,
Except with his own lonely moods
    The blackbird holds a colloquy.

Over the broad hill creeps a beam,
    Like hope that gilds a good man's brow;
And now ascends the nostril-stream
    Of stalwart horses come to plough.

Ye rigid Ploughmen, bear in mind
    Your labour is for future hours:
Advance—spare not—nor look behind—
    Plough deep and straight with all your powers!

Poetry was merely an occasional occupation to Alfred Domett; he was, nevertheless, professedly a disciple of Browning, who made him the Waring of the poem, a fact which gives him, perhaps, a moment's fictitious interest in a brief study of Victorian poetry. His poetic gift was real but slightly tended, and fell into neglect in a life of politics. His *Flotsam and Jetsam*, however, deserves some remembrance, and the following will serve to show that his discipleship to the great poet who was his friend was not wholly a vain one.

INVISIBLE SIGHTS

" So far away so long—and now
   Returned to England ?—Come with me !
Some of our great ' celebrities '
   You will be glad to see ! "

  .   .   .   .

Carlyle—the Laureate—Browning—*these !*
   These walking bipeds—Nay, you joke !—
Each wondrous power for thirty years
   O'er us head-downward folk

Wrapt skylike, at the Antipodes,—
   Those common limbs—that common trunk !
'Tis the Arab-Jinn who reached the clouds,
   Into his bottle shrunk.

The flashing Mind—the boundless Soul
   We felt ubiquitous, that mash
Medullary or cortical—
   That six-inch brain-cube !—Trash !

The third of the poets mentioned, T. E. Brown, is of a wider popularity and a more distinguished talent than the others. His poems have remained in print and still find many readers, and the reputation of his best work is likely rather to be increased than diminished by time. A shy and scholarly figure, he was a good democrat in his poetry and wrote of humble lives without condescension and yet rather from a sympathetic seclusion than as a poet of the people. Perhaps his mind was the one of his generation in which Browning's influence worked to most considerable purpose, though it would be at least as true to say in justice to a genuine but limited poet that his was a striking instance of a smaller poetic endowment working under the same technical instincts as the greater. In his work we find a rhapsodic note of lyricism, a sense of dramatic antithesis, a fondness for elliptical argument, all of which are in Browning's habit. Brown's touch in his longer poems may not be as firm as the master's, which is merely to say unnecessarily that he was not as great a poet as Browning, but in his shorter pieces he could often score a success in a manner that Browning himself could hardly have used more effectively, in evidence of which *Salve* may be given.

To live within a cave—it is most good;
    But, if God make a day,
    And some one come, and say,
" Lo ! I have gather'd faggots in the wood ! "
    E'en let him stay,
And light a fire, and fan a temporal mood !

So sit till morning ! when the light is grown
    That he the path can read,
    Then bid the man God-speed !
His morning is not thine : yet must thou own
They have a cheerful warmth—those ashes on the
    stone.

The single exception that has been mentioned to the generalisation, that Browning had little effect upon the work of his greater contemporaries, is Coventry Patmore. Of all the great poets of his time he has hitherto been by far the least generally understood and appreciated. His most celebrated poem, *The Angel in the House*, is full of material that lends itself easily to light censure, and, however tenderly the poem may be lit by intermittent beauties, it must be allowed that the general scheme is, on the whole, at least a poetic indiscretion, which in the case of so ambitious a structure is to write down failure. But the Patmore of the *Odes* is another matter, and here we have a poet who can find his company only among the greatest of his time. And the manner of these *Odes* is one of great range and variety,

not at all the range and variety of a facile
imitative gift, but notably of original poetic
invention. It may, in view of his relative
reputation, and, indeed, of his relative stature,
sound a preposterous thing to say, and I admit
that I say it only to stress an argument, but if
the work of a single poet alone had to be
chosen to survive in witness of the genius of
Victorian poetry in its many aspects, a by
no means frivolous case might be made for
Patmore's claim. It is true that many aspects
of the age's genius would then be recorded in
something a little short of their finest manifestation, though others could hardly ask for
more authoritative witness. But in no one
poet are the several aspects assembled at so
representative a level of expression. The pressure of Patmore's individual poetic energy was
not so great as that of Tennyson or Browning,
hardly as that of Morris or Arnold or Swinburne.
His spiritual insight at its most intense was as
revealing as that of any poet of his or, indeed,
of any age, but in his poetic life he did not
dwell as habitually at the centre of creative
energy as those his great contemporaries.
There was too often something occasional in
his work, not in the mere choice of subject,
but in his imaginative relation to the subject
when chosen, to allow him poetic constancy of

the first order. And that is, perhaps, on the whole, the reason why, advancing as his reputation continues to be in the best critical opinion, it is, and is likely to remain, a little below that of the highest of his time. While this is so, however, it is also true that there was very little in the manifold achievement of Victorian poetry that Patmore did not at some time or another come to by the entirely personal movement of his own genius. This copiousness in his talent was a thing quite distinct from Swinburne's sublime virtuosity, more lonely in its origin and much more far-reaching in its influence.

One of the most remarkable poetic affinities of recent times is to be found between the genius of Francis Thompson and that of Alice Meynell. However much these two poets may have resembled each other in spiritual temperament no two could differ more decidedly in poetic method. Thompson, whose manner is piled up in magnificence, exuberant in trailing and intricate imagery, drenched with every perfume and stained with every dye that he can extract from language at the very pitch of eloquence, is in his diction the flushed and almost breathless consummation of all the more luxuriant tendencies in Victorian verse. Alice Meynell, on the other hand, with her diction

so chaste and disciplined and exact, her imagery
so frugal and unadorned, is a rarefied incarna-
tion of the grave magic that the genius of
Matthew Arnold had caught from the seventeenth century, a century which in so far as it
worked upon Thompson did so rather in its
florid ecstasy.   And yet the poet from whom
both Thompson and Alice Meynell derived more
clearly than any other among the Victorians
was Patmore, and it was no doubt a consciousness that they inherited widely divergent strains
from a common parentage that accounted in
some measure, at least, for their responsiveness
to each other, not merely in sympathetic
appreciation, but in their essential poetic
natures.   For Patmore, too, knew the seventeenth century, and more consciously than did
any other poet of his time, and he knew it
both in its serene logical enchantment and in
its almost demoniac spiritual fervour.   He wore
both manners with a Victorian difference, but
he could wear them, and independently of each
other.   Of the first this is an example—*Vesica
Piscis*.

In strenuous hope I wrought,
And hope seem'd still betray'd;
Lastly I said,
" I have labour'd through the Night, nor yet
Have taken aught;
But at Thy word I will again cast forth the net ! "

And, lo, I caught
(Oh, quite unlike and quite beyond my thought,)
Not the quick, shining harvest of the Sea,
For food, my wish,
But Thee !
Then, hiding even in me,
As hid was Simon's coin within the fish,
Thou sigh'st, with joy, " Be dumb,
Or speak but of forgotten things to far-off times to
     come."

And of the second, this—

.   .   .   .

O, Death, too tardy with thy hope intense
Of kisses close beyond conceit of sense ;
O, Life, too liberal, while to take her hand
Is more of hope than heart can understand ;
Perturb my golden patience not with joy,
Nor, through a wish, profane
The peace that should pertain
To him who does by her attraction move.
Had all not been before ?
One day's controllèd hope, and one again,
And then the third, and ye shall have the rein,
O Life, Death, Terror, Love !
But soon let your unrestful rapture cease,
Ye flaming Ethers thin,
Condensing till the abiding sweetness win
One sweet drop more ;
One sweet drop more in the measureless increase
Of honied peace.

These are not seventeenth-century verse, but
they are striking examples of Victorian verse

worked upon by two main influences from the seventeenth century, and they bring Patmore representatively into line on the one hand with the " florid and flowing schemes " of Tennyson, and on the other with the " stiffer movement and graver tones " of Arnold. And that outside both these he was also subject to the instincts of Browning's characteristic manner the following poem will show.

> A woman is a foreign land,
>   Of which, though there he settle young,
> A man will ne'er quite understand
>   The customs, politics and tongue.
> The foolish hie them post-haste thro',
>   See fashions odd and prospects fair,
> Learn of the language *How d'ye do ?*
>   And go and brag they have been there.
> The most for leave to trade apply
>   For once at Empire's seat, her heart,
> Then get what knowledge ear and eye
>   Glean chancewise in the life-long mart.
> And certain others, few and fit,
>   Attach them to the Court and see
> The Country's best, its accent hit,
>   And partly sound its Polity.

VIII

In the scheme of the present study no more need be said of the technical side of Victorian poetry, nor need anything at all be said of such specific matters of technique as rhyme, syllabic equivalence, stanzaic structure, or prosodic abstractions, beyond to remark that in all these things, although there is an infinite variety of practice, the Victorian age added little that was essential to the history of English poetry. Perhaps, indeed, it was inevitable, and in no wise to be regretted, that it should add nothing. Further, to examine the rhythmic achievement of the age would be to examine at length the work of each individual poet, even to present a complete edition of each individual poet's works, since the rhythmic life of each poet is at once as individual and as incalculable as are the gait and gesture of a man. It has been my purpose, rather, to consider the many tendencies that display themselves in the diction of Victorian poetry, since in and through these can be most clearly marked the distinguishing characteristics of any poetic age. In doing this I have necessarily sometimes foreshadowed what there will be to say in the later part of this study, where the content matter of Victorian poetry will be considered, and where some poets will be dealt with whom it did not seem necessary to mention at this earlier stage of the argument. What cannot be told of the technical characteristics of Victorian poetry from the examples of Tennyson and Browning and those other poets that we have considered cannot be told at all.

Part II

I

Nothing is easier than for one age to be shallow and arrogant about the spiritual and intellectual preoccupation of another. To active minds, even the most cynical among them, life is such an urgent and absorbing business, so desperately charged with significance, that it is easy enough to suppose that contemporary methods of approach to it are the only wisely chosen ones, and this particularly in contrast with those of an immediately preceding age. I do not know that any critic of to-day thinks that Homer was a liar or a fool because he believed, or professed to believe, in the hierarchy of Zeus and the enchantment of the Sirens, or complains that Shakespeare was a credulous ghostmonger, or that Shelley, in holding that the world could be satisfactorily governed by a quixotic political idealism, was only a little less inept than Machiavelli, who thought that it could be redeemed by political craft. We find no difficulty in accepting Homer and Shakespeare (who, by the way, is just as likely to have actually believed in the appearance of ghosts as not, and who made fairies real, when most modern writers can do nothing but make them silly) on their own terms in their relation to life. If we understand the functions of poetry we are not the less moved by Milton's description of the creation of the world because we no longer believe that it happened in that way, and I suppose there would be none among us found with temerity enough to suggest that Milton himself did not believe it and that he was setting his story down idly without conviction. In all these instances we are willing to admit that it is not the creed that matters, but the faith and passion with which it is held, and we will allow the poets any conclusions they like so long as we are persuaded of their own imaginative good faith. And yet this generosity is not always found when the conclusions happen to be those of an age against which our own lives are partly passed in reaction, and many honest critics who would call Homer neither liar nor fool are misled into calling Tennyson both.

Among Victorian poets Tennyson is at the centre of a philosophic life against which the intellectual habit of our own time is often in active opposition. This being so, much may be excused to the excesses of self-interest, and we can make some allowance, for example, for a current mood that thinks it rather indelicate to speak about mere goodness, when it reprimands a mood of yesterday that thought goodness a very simple and natural thing to talk about. But to make allowances for it is not to approve it, and it is about time for us to stop making ourselves ridiculous by talking about the great Victorians as though they were lost in a fog of superstition and prudery and moral timidity.* We need not abase our-

* Mr. Harold Nicolson's recently-published book on Tennyson illustrates my point. The book is an acute and, in nearly every respect, a sympathetic piece of thinking, but it is coloured by the circumstance, due to the reaction of which I have spoken, that Mr. Nicolson often thinks Tennyson intellectually very little apples. And in this respect—in this respect alone—he patronises Tennyson, and the result is unfortunate, not for Tennyson but for Mr. Nicolson. It really will not do to say that Tennyson was an exquisite lyric poet but a blundering old prig intellectually. Tennyson's intellectual approach and expression were not Mr. Nicolson's, and it is perfectly right for Mr. Nicolson to stand for his own. But he should have remembered that Tennyson was not only the lyrist that he admits him to be, but, when all is said and done, a giant among the minds of a remarkable age. Had he done this he would not have marred what is otherwise a very beautiful piece of critical exposition

selves before them, but, also, we need not talk
as though the dawn of intellectual candour
had broken somewhere about 1900. It is all
really such a little matter, the difference, just
a change of deportment, that is all. At many
modern tables, if you should speak of goodness
everybody blushes or simpers, if, indeed, there
is not some very bold spirit to rebuke you
openly. But if you speak of the other thing
everyone is happily at ease and you realise
how fearlessly we to-day are facing the truth
about life. At our grandmothers' tables it was
different. The freedom of to-day would have
caused consternation there, but our own inhibi-
tions would have been unintelligible. There
have been loss and gain both ways, and the
balance remains about the same. After all, it
is just as unaccountable to be discomposed by
Tennyson when he makes Galahad say

> My strength is as the strength of ten
> Because my heart is pure. . . . . .

as it is to be discomposed by Mr. Masefield
when he makes Saul Kane say

> I'll bloody him a bloody fix,
> I'll bloody burn his bloody ricks. . . . .

In this study of the substance of Victorian
poetry, therefore, we will dismiss at once any
suggestion that we are dealing with a period

I

of intellectual adversity. Tennyson and the group of poets who represented in some degree or another Tennyson's mood were neither keener nor duller in the wits than the poets of other ages, and since we go to poetry not for what we can learn from it, but for an invigoration of the mind towards the establishment of our own learning, it need not trouble us that Tennyson's point of view happened in many ways to be one that is peculiarly antipathetic to our own.

II

There would seem to be two different kinds of material upon which the poetic faculty can be employed. The old distinction of subjective and objective has become loose in usage, as is the fate of all definitions, but it is not a bad one for working purposes. If in the discussion of æsthetics we begin to qualify our definitions too exactly we are apt to finish up in a world of unintelligible refinements. Words when used in argument have not the same quality and should not be expected to perform the same functions as they do in poetry, qualities and functions the nature of which has already been suggested. All modern moralising, for example, has tended towards the rejection of such plain words as good and bad. We no longer speak of a good man and a bad man as the Old Testament and Bunyan did, and we can show very good reasons for the rejection. Psychology has taught us that it is quite unsafe to call anyone just good or bad and leave it at that, and it is one of the achievements of modern literary art, particularly in the drama and in fiction, to explore with great subtlety the gradations by which good and bad merge into each other in a single character. Nevertheless, after such analysis has exhausted itself with every ingenuity, there remain the words good and bad, and in the ordinary communication of ideas we do know, with more or less precision, what is meant when someone of normal intelligence tells us that so and so is a good man or a bad man. And so with such words as objective and subjective in the consideration of æsthetics. It is perfectly true to say that no subject matter controlled by a poet's art can ever be wholly one or the other, but it is also true to say that if a narrative poem like *The Lay of the Last Minstrel* is spoken of as being objective in nature, and a philosophical self-analysis like *The Prelude* as being subjective, we know clearly enough what is meant. If we go further and say that in a work such as *King Lear* we get the two natures perfectly combined in one organism, we are still talking without wilful obscurity, and we are explaining in a rough and ready way, and yet in a way that is, perhaps, as good as any other, why it is that a work like *King Lear* shows poetry in its highest and most comprehensive exercise. It is not that *The Lay of the Last Minstrel*, in presenting a graphic pageant of life external to Scott's own personal experience, has nothing of that experience woven into it, nor is it that *The Prelude* in its constant concern with Wordsworth's own spiritual processes has no observation towers that look out on to the open road. But the external pageantry on the one hand and the self-analysis on the other are quite clearly the predominant motives of the respective poems, just as they are perfectly mated in *King Lear*, where there is at once everything of the vivid perception of a detached life that can be found in Scott, and everything of deep spiritual responsibility that can be found in Wordsworth, the one now transfigured by passion and the other lit by a new imaginative variety. With so much definition, therefore, the terms subjective and objective may be used for our present purposes.

Scott's poems are the best examples in English of poetry that is purely, or almost purely, objective. And the neglect of more recent criticism has, I suspect, left them still

in the possession of the affections of many
readers. They are not only the best of their
kind, they could not very well be better. The
finer narrative art of Chaucer, suffused as it
was by a much more personal contact with its
content matter, stands really in æsthetic significance, apart from the question of individual
genius, with the art that produced *King Lear*.
In the Victorian age the art of Scott found
its inheritors, and, although the schoolmasters
have done their best to kill *The Lays of Ancient
Rome*, Macaulay was no bad practitioner in a
kind of which we are foolish to speak slightingly
because it does not happen to be the highest.
If we can forget the class-room and put pre-
judice aside, and keep our sense of values clear,
there is something amiss with us if we do not
thrill to passages, of which there are many in
the *Lays*, such as

> Then out spake brave Horatius,
>   The Captain of the Gate :
> " To every man upon this earth
>   Death cometh soon or late.
> And how can man die better
>   Than facing fearful odds,
> For the ashes of his fathers,
>   And the temples of his Gods," . . . .

and

> Alone stood brave Horatius,
>   But constant still in mind ;
> Thrice thirty thousand foes before,
>   And the broad flood behind.

" Down with him ! " cried false Sextus,
    With a smile on his pale face.
" Now yield thee," cried Lars Porsena,
    " Now yield thee to our grace."

Round turned he, as not deigning
    Those craven ranks to see;
Nought spake he to Lars Porsena,
    To Sextus nought spake he;
But he saw on Palatinus
    The white porch of his home;
And he spake to the noble river
    That rolls by the towers of Rome.

" Oh, Tiber ! father Tiber !
    To whom the Romans pray,
A Roman's life, a Roman's arms,
    Take thou in charge this day ! "
So he spake, and speaking sheathed
    The good sword by his side,
And with his harness on his back,
    Plunged headlong in the tide. . . . . .

Macaulay was not by habit or any deep artistic
intention a poet at all, and the *Lays* are little
more than spirited footnotes to his history, a
point aptly made by Professor Hugh Walker
in his scholarly study of Victorian literature,
but as such they are the work of a very vivid
talent and have a secure if humble place among
the memorable poetry of their age.   There is
no work of the time exactly comparable to
Macaulay's unless it be that of William

Edmondstoune Aytoun, but the *Lays of the Scottish Cavaliers*, far from being without merit though they are, have no special characteristics that call for mention here.

All the greater poets of the age tried their hand at some time or another at objective narrative verse, but Morris alone among them made narrative a chief concern of his art. *The Life and Death of Jason, The Earthly Paradise* and *Sigurd the Volsung*,* together make up a body of narrative poetry by virtue of which it would be difficult to call Morris in this kind the inferior of anyone but Chaucer. Morris had not Chaucer's sense of character, nor his humour, nor, perhaps, the variety of his invention, but in pure narrative gift, the art of keeping the reader's attention fixed upon the progress of a long story, it is doubtful whether he is to be placed even below Chaucer himself. It is, however, when we call to mind that quality in Chaucer which, as I have suggested, gives his art something of the comprehensiveness that is supremely achieved in *King Lear*, that we feel Morris, great poet though he was, to have been definitely the less considerable man of the two. Morris loved the world of his invention, and loved it passionately, but

* It is unnecessary here to discuss the claim that would place *Sigurd* in the region of epic.

his narrative poetry is not quite authoritatively marked by his own spiritual agonies and exultations. In speaking of so noble a poet, and one so rich in pleasure-giving, one would say nothing that should savour at any distance of disparagement. Nor is Morris to be belittled because Chaucer was his master, not only by example, but by achievement. At the same time, in Morris's narrative poetry, however splendidly it may compel every other honour, there is to those who love it a perplexing something which leaves it short of the very highest. In a strange and impalpable way it seems as though he had withheld some last heart-beat from its creation. His claim, frequently made, that the writing of poetry was easy is not without some symbolic significance. It may have been that Morris was too happy a man to be quite among the very greatest poets. His verse stories leave us with a feeling that he is not utterly exhausted after the act of creation, that the figures of his invention, tender and virile though they are, remain outside the inner secrecies of his own emotion. There is, in fact, a larger preponderance of exclusively objective intention in his work than in Chaucer's, and by so much he means the less in the final poetic reckoning. This is not to forget that, by comparison with any narrative poet other than Chaucer, Morris's work is flooded with subjective passion, far beyond that of Macaulay or of Scott himself. In the earlier part of this study I have suggested that Morris really lived in the world of his stories more actually than in the nineteenth century, and that is, I think, the truth. But his capacity for imaginative life at all, immense though it was, had always just a strain of decorative facility that marked it a little apart from the constant imaginative pressure that we find in Chaucer. Morris told us magnificent stories, very moving and quick with heroic life, and to read them is to pass into a world of living and significant romance. But, remembering our own mortality, he has not the touch of revelation that was so easily Chaucer's, not quite the same breath of apocalyptic love.

The narrative work of the other great Victorian poets hardly calls for special consideration, being incidental to and of a part with their normal practice, not the result, as with Morris, of a specific artistic plan. But at this point a word may be said of the many dramas that were written during the age, in which we should expect from the nature of this form something of that unification which has been referred to in what has been said about Chaucer and *King Lear*. The Victorian poets as play-

wrights, and they nearly all tried their hands
at the craft, suffered from the radical disability
of having no living theatre in which to learn
their craft and in which to see their invention
come to full embodiment.　This is not the place
to discuss the reasons why it came about, but
the fact remains that when Tennyson began to
write the English theatre had long since driven
out the spirit of poetry, and continued to
enforce the exile during the whole of his long
life.　The waste of energy incurred by Tennyson and Browning and Morris and Swinburne
and Arnold, not to name a number of less
celebrated men, in the writing of plays (of the
succession of poets preceding them the same
thing could be said) is one of the tragic futilities
both of English literature and of the English
theatre.　It was a time when the actor had
achieved complete ascendency in the theatre
and when what he wanted was, not creative
poets whose works he could perform, but hack
playwrights who could serve the purpose of his
own histrionic virtuosity.　No more of this
need be said here, but the list of Victorian
plays written by men of great poetic gifts is
a pathetic witness of the indomitable aspirations of the English genius towards drama
and of the shameless indifference through long
periods of the theatre towards those aspira-

tions. What these men might have done in a
fortunate theatre cannot be said, but in view
of the very imperfect evidence available it
would be quite unsafe to say of any one of
them that he had not the gifts that would
have served a great theatre greatly. In the
event, their dramas were, for the most part,
little more than elaborated lyrics thrown arbitrarily into an inert dramatic form. That is
to say, lacking the theatre, and the formative
influence of the theatre, the objective quality
which is the first essential of drama never
came into full play at all. Shakespeare, as I
suggested above, was a skilled playwright
because he had this objective faculty in a
measure only equalled, perhaps, by Homer,
and a great playwright because he impregnated
it with a subjective sense of equal supremacy.
But, whereas it needs a subjective sense to
make a great drama, drama of sorts can come
to a kind of life in the theatre through the
objective faculty alone, while without the
objective faculty you cannot have drama which
will hold the stage at all. And it was the
opportunity to develop that objective sense in
dramatic terms that was denied the poetic
genius of the Victorian age, as it had been
denied the poetic genius since the passing of the
Restoration comedies. So that anything that

is worth saying about the drama of the Victorian poets will be covered by the consideration of their poetry in general, and we may dismiss the specifically dramatic intention in it.

III

The point of attack chosen by most of Tennyson's detractors is the *Idylls of the King*. Detraction is ultimately a very inconsiderable force in the world, being exposed readily enough by the minds that know anything of the thing against which it is directed, and being of no consequence either way in its action on minds that know nothing of it. People who really read Tennyson can readily enough rebut the unthinking and often envious charges that are made against him, while it does not matter what effect these may have upon the people who do not read him at all. There is, nevertheless, in the evolution of a poet's reputation the necessary sifting from time to time of the evidence and a revaluation of the old judgments. The reaction against Tennyson that set in, as with all poets, for a period after his death, discovered many faults in his work, which clearly enough were faults, but it has allowed these far too great an importance in the general estimate of his poetry.

The common opinion, even the common critical opinion of some authority, that has been expressed in recent years about the *Idylls of the King* is a striking instance of this lack of balance and generosity. In the first place, we have been told over and over again that Tennyson emasculated Malory, that the new poet's Arthur was a Victorian gentleman reflecting the stiff glories and virtues of the Prince Consort's train, not the fiery warrior with a vigorous paganism shining through his Christian professions that lives in the pages of the old chronicler, and that the ladies of the *Idylls* have become stultified by the proprieties of a later court than Guinevere's. Setting aside the sneer implied by the use of the figure of Victorian gentility, a sneer that really bears far less examination than its agents may suppose, the charge is a true one, but it is difficult to see why it should be held to be very damaging to Tennyson. It may be readily allowed that his world, his sense of character, and his ideals of conduct, were not precisely, or even approximately, those of Malory, but I am not aware that he ever claimed that they were, or that in using the figures of Arthurian legend he was not as entirely justified in making his own interpretation as Malory had been in his own time in making his. Nothing is sillier in criticism than to come to an artist's presentation of a legendary, a romantic, or even an historical figure with an already fixed idea of what that presentation should be. The evidence about these things in almost every case leaves the way open to a dozen conclusions, any one of which may carry conviction so long as the artist is capable of creative singleness of heart. We are really impertinent if we demand that Tennyson should make of Arthur and Enid and Geraint and Lancelot and Guinevere and Merlin and Vivien something that squares with our anterior impressions gathered from Malory. All we are justified in demanding is that Tennyson shall give them life which would convince us of its reality had we never heard of them before. If it be argued that in that case Tennyson might just as well have invented a *personnel* of his own, the answer is that the poet since the beginnings has always, and justly, felt himself to be at liberty to draw upon the common stock of legend and history so that he may profit by the appeal made by a familiar setting and invest his creation with the elemental vitality that comes from association. When the Greek audiences went to see a new tragedy by one of their masters they knew beforehand that they would be shown a *dramatis personæ* with whose existence they were already familiar, and so the poet started off with the advantage of having an audience that took it for granted that the people of his play were really alive. But the gain carried with it for him no obligations, or, at least, none that he would not as a matter of course instinctively fulfil. That is to say, provided he did not positively turn the accepted tradition inside out he was not only allowed to make what new reading of it he liked, but he was actually expected by his audience to do this. And so it was with Tennyson in his *Idylls*. Had he made Arthur a lecherous bandit, or Enid a nagging vixen, or Lancelot a saintly anchorite, or Guinevere an evil light-of-love, then we could have complained with justice that he should have found other names for his creations. But he did none of these things. In their central nature the figures of his *Idylls* retain the essential characteristics that had belonged to them from the legends of the old days, and it is only in his modifications of these, often it may be readily admitted emphatic in character, that Tennyson reflected his own instincts and the spirit of his age.

To acknowledge the fitness of those modifications is as much the obligation of fair criticism as it is not to overstate them. It is true that every now and again we get a line or a phrase touched by the fashion of the moment that now seems a little grotesque to us, in the same way that at our particular range of time the bonnets and antimacassars of our grandmothers seem a little grotesque.* But in themselves these touches are not really odd, but only twigs, as it were, that have lost their sap in the larger spread of timber, as will happen in every permanent body of poetry. When we read that Geraint withheld punishment from the dwarf through " pure nobility of temperament," that he was " a little vext at losing at the hunt," when we hear that Vivien in her dissembling put on the appearance of " a virtuous gentlewoman deeply wrong'd " we may be amused for a moment. But the then current idiom of chivalry was not really any more absurd than the more ancient one of false traitors and perfect knights

* It is interesting to hear that the dealers are anticipating the moment when such things will become criterions of taste for the dilettante. Warehouses are being stocked for the new demand that may arise at any moment for rooms adorned by horsehair furniture.

and fair damsels, and, in any case, we lose our
sense of proportion if on the strength of it we
make a commotion about Tennyson's intellectual provincialism. These things, when
they are all of them accounted for in his
work, amount to the merest accident of an
occasional gesture in the whole general bearing
of the man, and in some kind, if not precisely
in that kind, they can be matched in every
poet. With more claim to attention than
these trivialities are lines something of the
same kind but of a deeper purport, such as
those when Merlin speaks of the king as

> O true and tender ! O my liege and king !
> O selfless man and stainless gentleman, . . .

" Stainless gentleman " has a certain poetic
flatness to our ears which it had not for
Tennyson and his readers. To-day it is not
supposed to be good form to speak about a
man being a gentleman at all, and democracy
no longer encourages us to think about a man
being a gentleman at all. We are all now
(at least we all may be) nature's gentlemen,
and much may be said for the doctrine.
Tennyson was part of a society where the
aristocratic distinction was not merely a
reality in fact, but one acknowledged intellectually, and the more we see of the world

K

the less certain can we be that any one stage
in social development is demonstrably better
than another. " Change is the law of life on
earth," says Mr. Gosse, and each generation may
suppose that the change is for the better, though
one may to-day, for example, meet very liberal-
minded and generous people who can make
out a very good case for a return to feudalism.
But we can cut the argument short by saying
that when Tennyson (or Merlin) spoke of
Arthur as being a " stainless gentleman " he
was being neither a prig nor a sycophant.
He might sing that

> Kind hearts are more than coronets,
> And simple faith than Norman blood. . . .

but there was also room in his scheme of
things for the specific distinction that saved

> O true and tender !   O my liege and king !
> O selfless man and stainless gentleman. . . .

from being merely tautological. And if it
comes to that, Tennyson here was nearer than
some of his critics to the spirit of Malory. It
is well enough to be of our time in matters of
social faith and to use the world as we find
it. To be doctrinaire in politics is mostly to
be futile, but habits of expediency which are
bred by trying to make the best of social

schemes at the moment should be dropped when we turn to the criticism of poetry.

If we dismiss these petty difficulties of manner, we shall find that in their main construction the *Idylls* present a life which is very unlike that which is suggested by their detractors. The anæmic and Gilbertian curates and schoolmarms who are supposed to people the poems in a pleasant Sunday afternoon atmosphere have no being at all when we come to examine the poems themselves. Taking Tennyson by himself, without reference to Malory or any other source, we may surmise that the men of the poems, the very Galahad and Lancelot and Bedivere and Geraint of Tennyson's creation, that is to say, would have displayed a decision of character and a strength of arm that would shake some of the long-eared critics out of their complacency and perhaps afford them a little wholesome exercise. And if anyone thinks that he could behave by any but the strict rules of chivalry in the presence of Tennyson's Guinevere there is something amiss with his schooling. If no better evidence can be advanced for Victorian effeminacy and prudery and coxcombry than the *Idylls of the King* the charge must go by the board. Finally, in this respect we need hardly defend Tenny-

son because he sometimes chooses to point a
moral as well as to adorn a tale, as when in
the middle of the Enid story he breaks off
with

> O purblind race of miserable men,
> How many among us at this very hour
> Do forge a life-long trouble for ourselves,
> By taking true for false, or false for true;
> Here, thro' the feeble twilight of this world
> Groping, how many, until we pass and reach
> That other, where we see as we are seen. . . .

This practice has always been and will always
remain a prerogative of poetry and it is not
purism but frivolity of intellect that objects
to it.

The actual poetic achievement of the *Idylls*
is very great. That as a group they have no
architectural unity is true, but they have never
professed such unity. As separate stories they
are graphically, and often very poignantly
told, with innumerable touches of great felicity.
They are pervaded by Tennyson's descriptive
gift and yet it is always closely woven into
the imaginative texture and hardly ever indulged (as it was often by even so great a
poet as Swinburne, for example) for its own
sake. When Geraint comes to the town of
the sparrow-hawk where

In a long valley, on one side of which,
White from the mason's hand, a fortress rose;
And on one side a castle in decay,
Beyond a bridge that spann'd a dry ravine:
And out of town and valley came a noise
As of a broad brook o'er a shingly bed
Brawling, or like a clamour of the rooks
At distance, ere they settle for the night. . . .

the fortress is not merely an effective piece of
decoration in the poem but part of its essential
life, just as is the shoal

Of darting fish, that on a summer morn
Adown the crystal dykes at Camelot
Come slipping o'er their shadows on the sand. . . .

and when Geraint rides

into the castle court,
His charger trampling many a prickly star
Of sprouted thistle on the broken stones. . . .

the image is hardly less at the centre of things
than Shelley's superb "blue thistles bloomed
in cities," of which it is inevitably, but finely,
reminiscent. Geraint's splendid challenge to
Edyrn's labourers, beginning "A hundred
pips eat up your sparrow-hawk," Yniol's
beautiful iteration of the refrain in Enid's
song, "Our hoard is little but our hearts are
great," Lancelot's discovery to Lavaine on
their approach to Camelot, "Hear, but hold
my name Hidden, you ride with Lancelot of

the Lake," are but casual instances of the
abounding poetic energy that informs the
poems. Nor are there wanting yet greater
triumphs of the imagination, things at the
very heart of poetic mastery. Geraint's self-
imposed penance never to ask Enid the significance of the accusation which he supposed
he had heard her make against herself is a
master-stroke of vision of which the dramatic
genius of Shakespeare himself might have been
proud, while I know of no moment in all
English poetry more surging with the tides
of tragic and heroic beauty than that in which
the great Arthurian epic comes to its close,
with the throwing of Excalibur back into the
Cornish water.

> So flash'd and fell the brand Excalibur :
> But ere he dipt the surface, rose an arm
> Clothed in white samite, mystic, wonderful,
> And caught him by the hilt, and brandish'd him
> Three times, and drew him under in the mere. . . .

The power of visualisation here is tremendous.
The lines are charged with a mystery that has
in it nothing that is inexact or nebulous, and
we see not an enchanted pool of a romantic
wonderland, but an actual water by the rock-
bound Cornish coast, the heart of a country
where was played out the immortal drama of
England's legendary chivalry. Here is the

beauty that transcends the beauty of pathos, the beauty of trembling and poignant vision such as we find in some great chorus of Euripides. By the evidence of such things, which are not seldom within Tennyson's reach, it is a very lean and jealous humour of criticism that can deny him a place among even the greatest.

A more debatable element in Tennyson's work may also be illustrated from the *Idylls*. When Arthur takes his last leave of Guinevere at the Almesbury convent he follows a touching recital of the founding and the character of the Round Table with an uncompromising indictment of Guinevere's sin. He announced separation as the only possible course to be taken in spite of his professions of indestructible love, and the assurance in which, perhaps, may be found just a grain of comfort for the detractors, " Lo ! I forgive thee, as Eternal God forgives." Guinevere accepts the impeachment and its consequences and in turn renounces her allegiance to Lancelot, not only in her life but in her heart, and the crux of the argument may be given in this passage from the king's parting charge—

" How sad it were for Arthur, should he live,
    To sit once more within his lonely hall,
    And miss the wonted number of my knights,

And miss to hear high talk of noble deeds
As in the golden days before thy sin.
For which of us, who might be left, could speak
Of the pure heart, nor seem to glance at thee?
And in thy bowers of Camelot or of Usk
Thy shadow still would glide from room to room,
And I should evermore be vext with thee
In hanging robe or vacant ornament,
Or ghostly footfall echoing on the stair.
For think not, tho' thou would'st not love thy lord,
Thy lord has wholly lost his love for thee.
I am not made of so slight elements.
Yet must I leave thee, woman, to thy shame.
I hold that man the worst of public foes
Who either for his own or children's sake,
To save his blood from scandal, lets the wife
Whom he knows false, abide and rule the house:
For being thro' his cowardice allow'd
Her station, taken everywhere for pure,
She like a new disease, unknown to men,
Creeps, no precaution used, among the crowd,
Makes wicked lightnings of her eyes, and saps
The fealty of our friends, and stirs the pulse
With devil's leaps, and poisons half the young.
Worst of the worst were that man he that reigns!
Better the King's waste hearth and aching heart
Than thou reseated in thy place of light,
The mockery of my people, and their bane."

This is a long instance to set out but it will
serve, not only for the immediate purpose of
discussion, but as a text for more general
consideration of a prevalent attitude in Victorian poetry of which Tennyson was the chief

exemplar. When every allowance has been
made for dramatic detachment, we cannot but
suppose that the passage quoted embodies a
belief to which Tennyson himself would have
subscribed, and it is difficult to get away from
the feeling that there is something radically
unsound in it. Every spectator of *Othello* must
have felt the impulse to leap on to the stage
and cry upon Othello to come to his senses
and realise that even if he cannot see that he
is being fooled by a villain he should at least
sit down and have the matter out with Desdemona. By his end Othello becomes a noble
and heroic figure, but, even allowing that he
discovers in the action what seem to him to
be sufficient grounds for the cruellest of his
suspicions, we can never feel in the body itself
of the play that his jealousy is anything but
contemptible. Had Shakespeare's method
been different, and had he concealed the truth
from us as he does from Othello, or had our
opinion inclined towards Desdemona's guilt
until the final revelation, we could still not
but have felt that she was tolerable company
at least compared with her termagant and
demoniac husband. But Shakespeare saw that
Othello was an immensely attractive figure as
an expression of life, without for a moment
insisting that he was an admirable figure on

the less elementary and yet in a sense lower
plane of conduct. That is to say, Shakespeare
could worship the nature in Othello as he
could worship all vivid life, and he could
present the moral limitations of that nature
with the deepest sympathy, even without any
implication of blame, but he was never in
danger of confusing them with moral virtues.
So far as there is any deliberate doctrine to
be found in Shakespeare's art, indeed, the
jealousy of Othello, even though it had been
proved to be as well founded as he himself
supposed, is shown to have been as disastrous
in its tragic destruction of character as the
blood-guilty ambition of Macbeth or the
drunken passion of Antony. But Tennyson,
although he was vitally interested in life, and
honest enough in his acceptance of the processes of life so far as he could interpret them,
had also certain abstract moral points of view
which he was apt to impose upon those processes in the course of creation. In this there
is a difference between the artistic purposes
of the two poets, a difference that had really
been slowly asserting itself in English poetry
from the end of the Shakespearean era until
Tennyson's time. It is a difference that on
the whole must definitely mark the later
poetry as less unadulterated in its creative

aims than the earlier, and it is a difference,
further, that has led to grave misconceptions
in the modern practice of the art.* It may
be worth while to analyse this difference a
little more closely.

It is clearly a mistake to suppose that moral
judgment did not come within Shakespeare's
scheme. Every one of his plays from the dark
and terrible pity of *Lear* to the light and
gracious revelry of *Twelfth Night* is charged
with moral judgment, but it is a judgment
that is strictly complementary to the action
of the characters within the play, and as
organically a concern of the poet's creative
function in the play as are the characters and
action themselves. In other words, the moral
judgment becomes inevitably a part of life
itself, and is an altogether profounder thing
than a merely abstract moral point of view.
And this, indeed, is one of the chief glories of
Shakespeare's art, as of the whole poetry of
his age, that it is intensely concerned with
life, with its moral consequences, but it is
hardly at all concerned with moral points of
view that are not directly the consequence of
life as it grows at the poet's bidding. That is

* That is to say, by causing a reaction that sup-
poses it to be outside poetry's function to have any
moral purpose whatever.

why we feel that Shakespeare loved Macbeth, whose moral conduct he must have condemned, no less than Rosalind, whose conduct he as certainly sanctioned. Both were a part of the life to which he brought the constant homage of genius, and although that genius could not but award disaster to one and happy honour to the other, there was no prefixed moral rule to be applied with a consequent alienation of affection in the one case and establishment of it in the other before the final reckoning was made. So soon after Shakespeare as Milton the difference begins to show itself. The explicit purpose of *Paradise Lost*, a purpose happily not too constantly kept in mind, is " to justify the ways of God to men," and with this implication that a standard has to be set up from the first whereby a man can be shown to be morally at fault and wilfully to have disobeyed rules laid down for his guidance, the abstract moral point of view is beginning to assert itself, and although Milton's art is sublime enough to make the disability of little account in the result, there is something less universal in the creative mood. Shakespeare gives us life, moulded to a temperament, it is true, but untrammelled by any other control, while Milton gives us life, still moulded to a temperament, but also

beyond that tested in some measure by a
morality that is intellectually fixed, and in
seeking to justify the ways of God—God being
only another word for that morality—Milton
inevitably fails to justify humanity as Shakespeare so triumphantly does. In imagination,
and fertility, and rhetorical invention, and
constructive grandeur, and even in passionate
realisation, Milton cannot be placed below
Shakespeare himself, but in understanding he
is below him, and this because he did not come
to life with a mind so open. By the time we
have come from Milton to Pope the difference
is emphasised. Shakespeare created, and his
creations carried their own doom with them.
Milton created, and his creations then had to
be judged by a morality that was held outside
the terms of their own being, as it were, and
the integrity of the art was a little less exact
in consequence. But the morality was one in
which Milton did passionately believe; he
would have gone to the stake for it, as many
brave men did go to the stake. Pope, too,
had a moral belief by which the creations of
his poetry had to be judged, but there would
have been no going to the stake for Pope in
its defence. The intellectual passion of Milton
had become an intellectual attitude in Pope,
and, since men make far more fuss about their

attitudes than their passions, Pope allowed his belief far more undisciplined play in his poetry than Milton had done. Milton moralised like the prophets of old, but Pope moralised like a modern schoolman. This is not to say that Pope in the process did not often achieve very good poetry, and he sometimes touched truth more profoundly, perhaps, than he knew. But when he tells us " whatever is is right " we are sure that he is making an extremely effective verse while we are not so sure that he is speaking out of his heart and not merely playing up to the philosophic exercises of Bolingbroke.

With Wordsworth the difference persists, but it has shifted its centre. His moral sincerity is no more in doubt than Milton's, and, indeed, his artistic control of moral judgment may be said to approach Shakespeare's more nearly than does Milton's. Between Shakespeare and Wordsworth, however, there still remains a great difference. Wordsworth, although subject to abstract moral convictions much more clearly than Shakespeare, is yet as unwilling as the great dramatist to impose them on his creations after the event, but the difference lies in the fact that with Wordsworth the whole substance of his creation is far more limited in

range than Shakespeare's, and precisely because it is from the first conditioned largely
by the moral conviction. That is to say that,
without any deliberate manipulating of his
art, Wordsworth by instinct brought into his
poetry only the kind of creations that were
not by their actual conduct, but in their
essential character, in keeping with his own
moral nature. The creative impulse led
Shakespeare no-one could tell from hour to
hour in what direction, and it was never
hampered in its movement by the poet's own
moral point of view. Milton's impulse, also,
could range far, but the issue, whatever it
might be, had to be tested by the same laws
in the end. With Pope, the administration of
the laws had become a more or less arbitrary
ceremony, very self-important as such cere-
monies are, and too often divorced from the
figures of any creative impulse at all. But
with Wordsworth the impulse never worked
happily outside the influence of the moral
nature by which its creations were ultimately
to be tried. And so, leaving Pope out of the
reckoning, since in these high matters, memorable poet as he was, he was of altogether
smaller stature, we may say that in the fitness
of the exercise of moral judgment Wordsworth stands with Shakespeare, but that, his

creation being governed largely by a moral
character already defined, instead of develop-
ing its own moral influences as it grows, it
is infinitely less various and complex than
Shakespeare's, while Milton approaches Shakespeare more nearly in range, but is less im-
pressive than either in his adjustment of
poetic to moral values.

We find, then, that Shakespeare was profoundly interested in an immense range of life
and not at all in moral points of view, that
Milton was interested in a range of life still
immense though less variously peopled, and
also passionately interested in moral points of
view, and that Wordsworth was as vitally
concerned with a range of life far more limited,
the very nature of which, however, absolved
him from the necessity of consciously applying
a moral point of view which had already been
allowed for by his art. In considering Tennyson's position in this matter we have to remember first that he was one of the very few great
English poets that have come to a very wide
popularity in their own time. Shakespeare
was popular, so far as the records of the
theatre of his day tell us anything, but he
was popular because he told a good dramatic
story on the stage and satisfied the needs of
theatre audiences. The moral grandeur with

which he invested his plays would in its
absence no doubt have left them far less
powerful in their contemporary appeal, but
it was not by this grandeur that primarily
he achieved his popularity. Milton was not
popular in his own lifetime at all, and Wordsworth, although he secured general fame
before his death, was never a voice for which
the multitude waited. Dryden and Pope had
great reputations in their time, but it was
rather among an exclusive and small literary
society than among the masses. Byron caught
the general ear by his gift of pure romantic
narrative, but he and Scott in their time were
satisfying the demand for good stories, which
has since produced the immense crop of
modern fiction. But Tennyson was in a
different case from all of these. Here was a
poet who was impressing, as no other poet in
England had ever done before, his moral and
philosophic views upon all sorts and conditions
of men, and this without using the great
circulating medium of the theatre or beguiling
with a tale. The time was not one of any
deeper intellectual or spiritual life than any
other, but one in which that life was more
diverse in its interests. Whether the edu-
cational and scientific and industrial develop-
ments that were going forward have been for

L

good or bad in the welfare of the community may be doubted, but there is no question that they were stimulating the average mentality of the country to a fresh activity. Religious and philosophic speculation, the adjustment of scientific discovery to faith, the economics of the new order, and the precise significance of the growing Imperial idea, these and other questions were the daily concern of the man in the street, and disputation was the common practice of nearly every hearthside. Perplexity followed on perplexity, and they were perplexities not only of private spiritual experience, but of public passion also. And upon these Tennyson's judgment was awaited with an unparalleled eagerness. Apart from the interest in his poetic genius, in the shaping power with which his art embodied his experience, there was a far-reaching concern with the actual nature of his conclusions. The poet was a prophet in the land, with an authority that he had not known since the old bardic days. Queues would form at the bookshops at the early hours of the morning on days when a new volume by him was to be published. And this touching faith in a poet's word was not held only by the simple-minded and bewildered generality who wanted ready-made solutions for their problems. It

was shared by working men and the great
leaders of science, by shrewd and liberal
scholars and by unlettered adolescents, by
the country squire and the stump orator, by
Calvinistic churchmen and free-thinkers, by
poets and the new Utilitarians, by the Queen
and the village pump, in short by all sorts
and conditions of men. When we remember
how representative an audience it was to
which Tennyson spoke we need hardly do
more than this to realise that the charge that
has sometimes been made against him of
intellectual shallowness or charlatanry is a
very ill-considered one. A religious or intellectual impostor may catch the easy ear of a
credulous public for a moment, pack revival
halls, or become a best seller, but a following
that included Jowett and Huxley and Rossetti
and FitzGerald and Francis Palgrave and
Butler of Trinity, Gladstone and Disraeli,
General Gordon and J. R. Green, George Eliot
and Stopford Brooke and Thackeray and
Tindall, not only as exceptional but as representative figures, was neither easy nor credulous, and when the last word of caricature
about Tennyson and his mantle has been said
the fact remains that in direct doctrine, as
apart from the subtler processes of poetry, he
had an influence upon the finest minds of his

age which can hardly be exaggerated. He
was an acknowledged as well as an unacknow-
ledged legislator.

This does not often happen to a poet and,
while we may be glad that now and again the
old office of poetry in the daily counsels of
the people should be renewed, it is well that
in the general run of things this should be so.
Nothing is more likely to turn a poet's head
than to be accepted as an oracle, and it must
be allowed that it turned Tennyson's head a
little. His was too fine a nature for the
effects to be very serious, and Mr. Nicolson
is inclined to overstate the case when he talks
of Tennyson's acumen in trimming his sails
to every fresh wind. The truth is that the
business of poetry and of ordered philosophy
are distinct things, and while many of us
think that in the end poetry has the more
persuasive voice of the two, as she certainly
has the more charming, it is not very good for
her to be flattered into the belief that she
can use both at will. And Tennyson was so
flattered. The moral judgment, the function
of which in Shakespeare's art, and Milton's
and Wordsworth's, we have discussed, became
with Tennyson as independent a preoccupation
as it had been with Pope, but with Tennyson it
was at once much more serious and much more

sincere and less witty in nature, and, in its divorcement from poetry, much more dangerous in consequence of this. This is by no means to say that Tennyson's moral pieces are never good poetry or that they are not very often durably convincing in their morality, but it is to say that he would often impose upon his poetry a moral judgment that was not a passionate one like Milton's or a sententiously dialectical one like Pope's, but an almost official one held with all the solemnity of official responsibility, and gathered as much from the abstract public opinion to which he in turn ministered as from his own brooding conviction. To say that Tennyson was dishonest in this is to say something that should not be said about so rare a poet and so single-hearted a man. It is not even as though the moral judgment to which he committed himself was ever one of which he could not quite sincerely say that he approved, and in further extenuation it must be remembered that, after all the talk about the waste tissue in Tennyson's work which came from his concern in this way with ephemeral moods and institutions, there is on actual examination very little of his poetry which makes wholly unprofitable reading to-day. But the trouble so far as it went was, it may be, that Tennyson was tempted into confusing moral opinions about particular things with a presiding moral judgment and to introduce these into a poetical context where they had no proper place. Milton's moral nature could assert itself over and above his poetical creation, and in so far as that was so he could be said to indulge a moral point of view in a way that made his sense of artistic fitness a little less fine than Shakespeare's. But Tennyson went beyond this, and not only allowed moral points of view sometimes to become the chief concern of poetry, in the manner of Pope, though Tennyson did it far more impressively, but he was also capable of allowing the pressure of moral points of view to lower the passion of his poetic creation in a way that Milton never did.

So it is that that passage at the end of *Guinevere* is fundamentally a betrayal of the very beautiful poetic life into which it intrudes. The moral point of view expressed is not only not inevitably Arthur's, that is to say, not an organic part of the poetry, it is not even a moral judgment pronounced by the poet upon his creation at the bidding of a vast natural impetus such as directed Milton in his judgments. Plainly the passage is introduced because Tennyson remembers that these views

about conjugal fidelity are likely on the whole
to be well received by the great audience that
is waiting for him. That they would, in fact,
be so received, that they were in keeping with
responsible opinion in the fabric of society,
and that they are, however successfully they
may sometimes be challenged, a comfortable
doctrine in the expediency of our modern life
with much to be said for it, that they are,
in short, moral views of some considerable
authority, are not sufficient excuses for Tennyson's misapplication of them. The point is
that, in a passage such as that given, Tennyson
was accepting a rule-of-thumb morality from
the social currency and not only passing it
off as a moral judgment welling up from the
deeps of poetic creation, but deceiving himself
into the belief that it was this. It was, in
effect, very much the sort of thing that Pope
had done, only Pope's shrewd common sense
kept him nearer to the fundamentals of moral
doctrine and saved him from the false evan-
gelical fervours that Tennyson was apt to
catch from the public congregations above
which he was so popular a figure. A congregation is, in fact, always a dangerous
venue for a poet, since even a congregation of
Jowetts and FitzGeralds cannot be wholly
clear of the demoralising atmosphere of the

revivalist meeting. It comes to this, that when Tennyson wrote that passage, although no doubt in argument he would have hotly defended the position advanced, he did not believe what he was saying with the full force of poetic conviction, and in consequence he marred a poem in which, for the rest, is an idyllic tenderness, set against an heroic background with perfect imaginative mastery. And the chief defect in Tennyson's poetry as a whole may be found to be of this nature. The flaws in *In Memoriam*, for example, one of the noblest elegiac poems in the language, nearly all have this common origin. The defect is very nearly the sum of the charge to be made against Tennyson's poetry, and it leaves the great body of his achievement but very little impoverished in character.

IV

This element in the management of the poetic function, which sometimes in Tennyson became a weakness, was one which left its traces upon the volume of Victorian poetry as a whole. It was, indeed, not a sudden phenomenon specifically of that age, since it had been gradually asserting itself in English poetry fo some generations, but it now became

for a considerable time an established part of
the tradition. That is to say, the interests of
poetry generally, although it was impossible
for them to explore more deeply the fundamentals of human nature than had been done
in the past, had by now become far more
various in their operations than they had
been. The great Victorian poets could achieve
no more of significant revelation than Shakespeare and Milton and Wordsworth, but they
did, as it happened, deal in their poetry with
a wider range of interests. The actual subjects
chosen by the Victorians for poetic treatment
far exceeded in number the subjects that had
been so chosen in any age before. One might
put it crudely and say that Tennyson and
Browning and Arnold, and some of the others,
wrote about every subject under the sun.
Tennyson is reported to have told a friend
that he would have written the Ode in praise
of Wellington, with all its political and imperial preoccupations, quite independently of
the claims of his function as laureate. A
Colonial Exhibition, the latest step in the
theory of evolution, the progress of the
feminist movement, a marriage in the royal
family, these things could move his emotions
with hardly less authenticity than the eternal
exultations and desires that were for him, as

they had been immemorially, the subject-
matter of poetry. When we remember what
vast tracts of even that common ground had
in different ages been left almost wholly
unexplored by poetry, we realise more fully
the catholicity of interest which now called it.
The great age of the Elizabethan lyric, for
example, hardly touched the resources of
nature as material for poetry, while with the
age of Pope love poetry passed with the last
artificialities of the later Carolines into almost
complete silence for a generation. And, again,
for a period of over a hundred years, between
the death of Vaughan and the coming of
William Blake, the note of religious mysticism,
with the exception of Christopher Smart's one
ecstatic moment, almost goes out of English
poetry altogether. If, remembering these
things, we then turn our minds to the Victorians, and have a sense of their poetic mood,
we at once realise that it would have been
almost inconceivable that any one of them
should have failed in the course of his usual
practice to write a great deal about all these
things, nature and love and religion, and we
find, in fact, that each one of them did so.
But in going beyond these and kindred subjects, as they habitually did, to more specific
and local interests for their inspiration, they

became, in a sense that no group of masters had been before, occasional poets.

It was fortunate that they brought to their office as such the best of their qualities, and did not reserve these alone for the inspirations more accredited by tradition, so that occasional poetry, in the Victorian age, very often became great poetry. In reading the poetry of no other age do we so often feel that a poet of first-rate endowment has, as it were, been hunting about for a subject. Occasional poetry conceived and carried out in the great manner had hitherto been almost wholly confined to personal addresses of compliment or condolence, and fustian as these mostly were there had been very noble exceptions. But with the Victorians the occasions were unconfined, and any one of the poets might at any moment produce a memorable poem, as it seemed, upon something that might catch his eye in the morning paper. If, by way of illustration, we were to take the titles of a hundred of Donne's poems and set them beside the titles of a hundred of Browning's, we should find that in external range the one would be, as it were, a small green isle and the other a very archipelago. I need not labour the point that this does not at all suggest that Browning was a greater poet

than Donne; it merely emphasises the fact
that Browning's age was far less concentrated
in its poetic attentions than was Donne's.
The result of which was that Victorian poetry,
with all its great central merits, all its loyal
assertion of the eternal elements, acquired a
certain scattered character, a certain disorder
in bulk, that leaves the essential spirit of this
age a little more than commonly difficult to
come at.

A further result was that a good deal of
Victorian work is of a lowered significance
when set beside work of corresponding eminence
in other ages. The moments of artistic surrender such as we find playing havoc with
Tennyson's poetry in such a passage as that
given from *Guinevere* were not uncommon in
the work of the age, though they often came
in another and less disastrous aspect. The
arbitrariness that so often governed—or left
ungoverned—the Victorian choice of subject,
could not but sometimes bring about a relation
of something less than the highest imaginative
urgency between the poet and the occasion
of his verse. In the general run of poetic
practice this did not necessarily mean an
entire failure of the spirit nor a total absence
of enchantment, but it did more often than not
make the thing created seem to be less in-

evitably an addition to the riches of English poetry. A great deal of the work of so admirable a poet as Mrs. Browning, for example, is heavily marked by this condition. Setting aside her obvious but unimportant technical deficiencies, we find in reading one long piece of hers after another that it "hath all the good gifts of nature" except indisputable evidence of its original necessity. A poem such as *An Island* sparkles with tender and expressive imagery—

> For all this island's creature-full
> (Kept happy not by halves),
> Mild cows that at the vine-wreaths pull,
> Then low back at their calves
> With tender lowings, to approve
> The warm mouths milking them for love.
>
> Free gamesome horses, antelopes,
> And harmless leaping leopards,
> And buffaloes upon the slopes,
> And sheep unruled by shepherds;
> Hares, lizards, hedgehogs, badgers, mice,
> Snakes, squirrels, frogs, and butterflies.
>
> And birds that live there in a crowd,
> Horned owls, rapt nightingales,
> Larks bold with heaven, and peacocks proud,
> Self-sphered in those grand tails;
> All creatures glad and safe, I deem.
> No guns nor springes in my dream!

And yet the whole has something of the

character of a despatch from a divinely gifted special correspondent. And the same thing may be said sometimes even of so spiritually immaculate a writer as Christina Rossetti. *Goblin Market* is a masterpiece, conceived out of a lovely nature and flawlessly executed, but if our minds go from it to Drayton or Herrick, with whom it has some affinity, we are aware not of a surer touch in the older poets but of a stricter visitation. *Under the Rose*, a triumph of delicately controlled power, has, very elusively here, the same suggestion of something occasional in its character. Perhaps the most notable instance of all is Edward FitzGerald's *Rubaiyat*,* and here we are on delicate ground, since we are speaking of not only one of the most celebrated poems of the age, but of one of the most remarkable. At first thought it might seem that of no poet could it less justifiably be said that in his principal life-work he was allowing any occasional or even any external influence to play upon his creative mood. Fastidious in judgment, of lonely intellectual pursuits, having not the slightest regard for contemporary fame, indolent rather than eager in

---

* I speak of this poem as though it were Fitz-Gerald's original composition, without reference to Omar, which for essential purposes it is.

creation and, far from seeking occasion for poetry, relieved when he could pass it by, as he generally could, and wholly unconscious of anything like a mission, FitzGerald might well have been the last poet in whom to look for the accidental quality of which we are speaking. And yet it is this accidental quality that keeps his *Rubaiyat*, so rich in memorable excellence, so splendidly contrived and so often universal in its nature, from being among the very greatest moral poems in the language. The circumstance that it took its form from Fitz-Gerald's oriental studies and is Persian in its machinery is of no consequence; Shakespeare was equally Shakespeare in the Roman world and mediæval legend and his modern England, and as much might be said for Morris in Fitz-Gerald's own time. Here was a poem that was essentially religious in character—that its doctrine was one of agnostic hedonism notwithstanding. For such a poem to come to the highest achievement possible to its kind, the first indispensable condition is an uncompromising faith, and this is what FitzGerald had not even in his own *dolce far niente*. There had once in English poetry been an age of faith, and there had once been an age of reason, but FitzGerald was of an age in which faith and reason were, in the life of the nation, for the moment inextricably confused, and when poetry addressed itself to rhapsodical belief—or unbelief if you will—as it did in the *Rubaiyat*, the seductions of reason were ever-present and the fervour of confession was embarrassed by the insinuations of argument. This did not much matter in *In Memoriam* or in the great part of Browning's work that was religious in texture, because here speculation was, for good or ill, very largely the explicit province of the poetry. But FitzGerald's design was not speculation, it was disclosure, and when this is so poetry should breathe the spirit of the labourer addressing his wife, " I'm not arguin', I'm a-tellin' of yer." If the reader should think it worth while, for comparative purposes, to turn up a forgotten but splendid poem, *Memorials of Mortality*, by Joshua Sylvester,* he will find an admirable example of faith in somewhat lugubrious but trumpet-toned poetic assertion. There is no arguing in Sylvester, it is all rhetorical and solemn revelation, wholly indifferent to its audience and unconscious of the possibility of denial. With FitzGerald there is an under-

---

* 1563–1618, the translator of du Bartas, and a prolific poet known to most readers by one lovely sonnet, but otherwise neglected far beyond his desert.

tone always of anxiety to carry opinion with
him, very indefinite in expression and yet
present clearly enough if our attention is
close. We do not complain about it; to do
so would be at once foolish and ungenerous.
But we are aware of it and we know that it
is in some subtle way, and perhaps uncon-
sciously, a concession to a mood of the time,
which, as we have seen, was a little antagonistic
to the most commanding kind of poetic fulfil-
ment. When we read—

> 'Tis all a Chequer-board of Nights and Days
> Where Destiny with Men for Pieces plays :
>   Hither and thither moves, and mates, and slays,
> And one by one back in the Closet lays.
>
> The Ball no Question makes of Ayes and Noes,
> But Right or Left as strikes the Player goes;
>   And He that toss'd Thee down into the Field,
> *He* knows about it all—He knows—HE knows !

we cannot but admire the masterly, indeed
the unforgettable way in which the philosophic position is set forth, nor can we deny
that the statement is fairly within the terms
of poetry. But in such notes as this, which
are frequent in the *Rubaiyat*, we detect a
certain faltering in imaginative faith, not
precisely in intellectual conviction about the
creed which is being expounded, but in the

M

spiritual exaltation that may lift any creed, whether it be sacramental and beatific as in Crashaw's *St. Theresa*, or stoic as in Emily Brontë's *Last Lines*, or inscrutably naturalistic as in Mr. Ralph Hodgson's *Song of Honour*, above the regions of debate to the very pinnacle of authority. When all these reservations have been made, there is enough virtue and to spare in Victorian poetry to leave it written as a new and glorious chapter in the most national of our arts, nor can spiritual ecstasy itself be wholly denied it, as *Dost Thou Not Care?* and many other poems by Christina Rossetti, Tennyson's *Crossing the Bar*, Browning's *Prospice*, and, dark though its conclusions be, Arnold's *Dover Beach*, and Mrs. Browning's *Weeping Saviour*, and Coventry Patmore's *Vesica Piscis*, to name half a dozen poems at a venture, can testify. But, considering the manifestations of poetry in that age as a whole, spiritual ecstasy was one of its least constant achievements.

V

In nothing did the Victorian genius justify itself more fully than in its love poetry. Love, a theme which, apart from the Augustan silence which was broken only by such stray productions as James Hammond's *Love Elegies*, has been constant in English lyric poetry, had never before been sung at one time with so many individual accents. In the poetry of speculative thought and religion the Victorian disintegration of mind may have led to a certain fluttered insecurity, a lack of the superb moral poise which distinguishes the Greek and the Miltonic epochs for example, when, no matter how individual the poet, the rules as to what was and what was not the proper material of poetry had some authority. It was not insignificant that whereas Browning, we feel, could pick up the subject for a long philosophic poem in a morning's walk, Milton took twenty years to deliberate his choice. But in love poetry the advantage, by the same conditions, was with the Victorians. The law about the matter would seem to have a strange streak of paradox in its nature. To take speculative religion and love as contrasting themes by way of illustration, it would appear that since speculative religion is a thing about which at no time can there be any sort of standard or finality in the human mind, it is on the whole better for the purposes of art that some such standard arbitrarily fixed should be commonly accepted. On the other hand, since love is a thing about which in its actual nature there is little or no change from age to age as between one man and another, it profits art when individual interpretations of love are as wide as possible in their variety. The Greek drama, the high noon of Italian painting, the seventeenth-century devotional school of English lyric, all these gained enormously in impressiveness because in the creation of each of them there was present to every artist a more or less fixed central authority which he recognised as being greater than any he could set up by his own unaided meditation. But in love the individual's authority is as great as any common authority can be, since love itself, as apart from thought about love, is the same in its essential nature, whatever measure of that nature may be given, to one man as to another, and so there is gain when that thought about love, as distinguished from love itself, is allowed the utmost freedom; and in this freedom the Victorian age in poetry is more personal than any that had preceded it. If we consider love poetry as a whole we shall find but an extremely small part of it is concerned with the fundamental ecstasy of love itself, with the adoration of the lover for the beloved in terms of ordinary experience and

not modified by special circumstance as it was,
for example, with Dante, and when it is so
concerned it necessarily changes hardly at all
except in verbal idiom from age to age. Love
poetry, for the most part, is concerned not
with love itself but with the lover's attitude
towards and contemplation of his love, in fact,
not with love so much as with thought about
love. And this thought about love from age
to age had in poetry been largely governed by
a common attitude prevalent at the time.
Shakespeare's *Sonnets*, and a few individual
lyrics by other men, are so well known to
every reader of poetry that it is difficult to
say how readily we could distinguish them
without their familiarity, but beyond these it
is safe to say of the great body of Elizabethan
love lyric, with all its superb singing quality
and varied command of imagery, that we
could never with any certainty tell one poet
from another by the nature of his attitude
towards his subject. And so in a later age,
although we may find one fashion contending
with another, the respective sides are governed
by their own rules and there is no reason why
the poet who wrote " Tell me not, sweet, I
am unkind " should not also have written
" Ask me no more where Jove bestows," or,
on the other hand, why the poet who wrote

Shall I wasting in despair
Die because a woman's fair . . .

should not also have written

Out upon you, I have loved
Two whole days together. . . .

With the return of love as a theme to
English poetry in the Romantic revival, there
was for a time no very decided movement
either towards a general character or away
from it. Wordsworth dealt with the subjective
love emotion but very rarely, it inspired but
a few verses of Keats's best work, Byron's
poetic rank would have been very little
affected if, with the exception of two or three
stanzas, he had not used the theme at all,
and, apart from Shelley, Landor is the only
other poet who contributed any considerable
love poetry to an age which was mostly concerned in other directions. Shelley's great
and personal love poetry stands by itself in
its time, as did Donne's at an earlier period.
But, generally speaking, it may be said that
in each age before the Victorians when love
poetry had been a common practice in English
verse it had been marked always by reference
to some general attitude, with the result that
although it had never been deficient in lyric
beauty it had been, apart from individual

exceptions like Donne and Shelley, definitely limited in its psychological interest. With the Victorians, however, the most striking thing in this matter is that every poet of any consequence wrote love poetry and wrote a good deal of it, and it is never possible for a moment to confuse the love poetry of one with that of any other. The specific nature of each poet's individual contribution could only be attempted in separate studies in detail of those poets and cannot be analysed in this brief study of general characteristics. But to read Tennyson's *Maud*, Browning's *Last Ride Together*, *A Woman's Last Word*, *A Pretty Woman*, and *The Lost Mistress*, to choose four of his representative love poems, Rossetti's *House of Life*, and Mrs. Browning's *Sonnets from the Portuguese*, Patmore's *Unknown Eros*, and Swinburne's *Dolores*, is to pass through a succession of moods as different as they can well be in character and having nothing in common save that their attention is turned to one centre. And there is no likelihood of time slowly investing this heterogeneous body of poetry with a common character as it has done with the love poetry of past epochs. No formula can ever be invented that shall include the social conscience and romantic tenderness of *Maud*, Browning's passionate but ruthless psychological subtlety, Rossetti's entranced voluptuousness, the proud surrender of the *Sonnets from the Portuguese*, Patmore's transfigured worldliness and Swinburne's enraptured embodiment of an abstract passion in a substantial image. In Victorian love poetry there is no dominant figure but that of love itself, but the theme is celebrated with an orchestral fulness that had never before been attained.

Coming, as they did, after Wordsworth and Shelley and Keats, it cannot perhaps be claimed for the Victorian poets that they added notably to the spiritual revelation of nature, but it can be said in their praise that they were nearly all of them endowed with a very graphic gift of exact observation of the natural world. Victorian poetry is alight with phrases in which a natural mood or object is set down with the most tender and vivid precision. Tennyson's planet of Love,

> Beginning to faint in the light that she loves
> On a bed of daffodil sky. . . .

Mrs. Browning's delicate landscape where

>   sheep are cropping
> The slant grass and daisies pale,
> And five apple trees stand dropping
> Separate shadows toward the vale. . . .

FitzGerald's

> strip of herbage strown
> That just divides the desert from the sown. . . .

Christina Rossetti's image, as telling as one of Marvell's, of the

> Green nest full of pleasant shade,
> Wherein three speckled eggs were laid. . . .

Browning's " pear hung basking over a wall," Arnold's

> Have I not pass'd thee on the wooden bridge
> Wrapt in thy cloak and battling with the snow,
> Thy face towards Hinksey and its wintry ridge. . . .

Patmore's

> The buried bulb does know
> The signals of the year,
> And hails far summer with his lifted spear. . . .

Morris's

> I know a little garden close
> Set thick with lily and red rose. . . .

and Rossetti's " ground-whirl of the perished leaves of hope," such things can be matched on almost any page of any considerable poet of the time. The age may have been not very much concerned with the interpretation of nature in Wordsworth's prophetic sense, but the easy mastery over such images as those just given gave to the poetry of the time a common background of rich and varied natural beauty, very bright in line and colour.

VI

Nothing is vainer than for criticism of poetry to suppose that it can give anything of the pleasure to be found in poetry itself. In making these notes about Victorian poetry, and in reading over again the work of the masters who wrote it, I am acutely aware how dismally inadequate any commentary upon such work must be. I am aware, also, that one could confront every generalisation that one makes with some modifying example; I have, for instance, since saying what I did about the love poetry of by-gone ages, been haunted by Bishop King's exquisitely personal and touching *Exequy* on his " dead saint." But these exercises have their times, and they are at least an occasion for refreshing memories that are apt to become a little dulled even for the most loyal and industrious of us. Further, abstract theorising about art at least does the art no harm and may sometimes serve it. No one is likely to read the *Morte d'Arthur* or the *Garden of Proserpine* or the *Scholar Gipsy* or

Pippa Passes with any more poetic delight for anything that he may find in this essay, but here and there a friendly mind may get a little pleasure of a real though less essential kind in considering for a moment, apart from the fundamental things of poetry that persist from one generation to another, what were the characteristics that distinguished an age, of which these are representative creations, from the other ages with which it has now taken an equal and immortal place.

Index

Poetry.

Romantic & classical as regards form
of verse: Br. most romantic: M.A. least.

Romantic & realistic as regards subj. matter

Romantic (i) love of the past.

(ii) love of the supernatural.

(iii) subjective

By the time we reach Mid-Victorian time
the things for which Wordsworth etc fought
have been accepted.

(iv) love of external nature.

Realistic.

(i) scientific observation of nature.

(ii) interest in social questions.

Br. is a romantic realistic.
takes romantic subject and treats it in
a realistic way. not as T. takes a
romantic subject & treats it in a
Victorian way. eg. King Arthur.